JOHNNY
LOGAN

THE TRUE STORY OF A SHAWNEE
WHO BECAME A U.S. SPY

A NOVEL BY
ALLAN W. ECKERT

Jesse Stuart Foundation
Ashland, Ky
2010

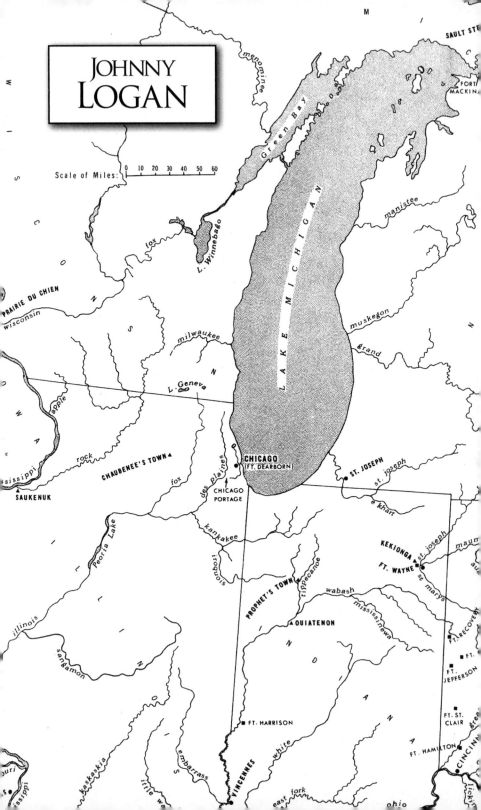

Ohio country and parts of Kentucky, Indiana and Michigan, showing the locations of major streams, towns and cities, Indian villages, forts, battle sites and other pertinent points.

To the memory of a fine American

W. D. "Bo" Randall

ISBN 1-931672-64-4

Cover Design by Brett Nance

Published By:
Jesse Stuart Foundation
1645 Winchester Avenue • Ashland, KY 41101
(606) 326-1667 • JSFBOOKS.com

The Shawnee Indian named Spemica Lawba — called by the whites Big Horn or, erroneously, Bright Horn, but who gained fame under the name of Johnny Logan — was a real person and this is the story of his life: the story of one of the greatest and most faithful Indian friends the white men ever had on the American frontier . . . and the only Indian buried with full United States military honors.

Many of the major incidents in Johnny Logan's life have been fully documented but, understandably, there are gaps in the story. In this book, in order to provide a smoothly flowing narrative of Johnny Logan's amazing life, the author has taken the liberty of filling these gaps with data believed to be factual but for which there is no known documentation. These additions have been made with considerable care and only after a very careful study not only of all the substantiated information about Spemica Lawba's life, but of the Shawnee culture and history of the period involved and the individuals involved. All of the major incidents described in the book are true; the author has taken license only with minor matters which neither affect nor alter history. Much of the dialogue is taken directly from historical records, but a certain amount has been created — always in keeping with the character of the individuals concerned and with the known data.

The Ohio Country referred to in the book includes all of the present state of Ohio and portions of eastern Indiana and southern Michigan. The Northwest Territory referred to is the region of mid-America that was the original Northwest Territory, encompassing Ohio, Indiana, Illinois, Michigan and Wisconsin and part of Minnesota.

Use of the Shawnee language and descriptions of Shawnee customs — and those of other tribes — come from historical records. The warfare, dances, games, sports, social activities and other aspects of Shawnee life depicted here are very closely documented.

All of the characters in this book, both Indian and white, were real people who lived the life and did the things they are portrayed as having lived and done. No fictional characters are included.

         — ALLAN W. ECKERT

Everglades, Florida
March 1983

CHAPTER I

December 2, 1774

OTH WOMEN in the wegiwa were silent now, each lost in her own thoughts, each feeling the resurgence of pain that their conversation had inspired. Their faces were expressionless, one middle-aged and prematurely etched with lines of suffering, the other young and smooth, uncommonly attractive, with the dim glow of firelight reflecting from the faint sheen of perspiration on her cheeks and forehead.

The great joy and anticipation that this day should have inspired was sullied, blunted by the terrible tragedy that had occurred less than two months ago, a tragedy that had changed them both, especially the older woman. On that day both of their husbands had been killed. In a way, the loss to the younger woman was the greater, for while the older woman had lost a husband, the younger woman had lost both a husband and a father, which is what the two men had been to her. The women were mother and daughter and their names were Methotasa and Tecumapese.

The latter lay on her side, propped up by one elbow, on the thick bison hide that protected her from the coldness of the hard-packed earth beneath. She wore no clothing but was covered by a soft, light coverlet of beautifully tanned hides of muskrats meticulously sewn together, the fur side against her skin. Tecumapese, not yet seventeen, looked at her mother who sat on a smaller fur mat nearby and in the midst of her own pain, both mental and physical, she experienced a great welling of sympathy, knowing that Methotasa would never again be the same. She was on the point of speaking to her when another spasm came, sharp and prolonged, and a barely audible sibilance escaped her as she sucked in a breath.

Methotasa's reverie broke and she turned her head. She reached out and placed a hand gently on her daughter's swollen abdomen. "Soon, Tecumapese," she said quietly, nodding. "Not yet, but soon."

Tecumapese smiled faintly and nodded in turn. "I know, Mother. He has had enough of the waiting."

That she should refer to her unborn child as male with such certainty was no surprise. There was no doubt whatever in her mind that this first child of hers would be a boy, not since the day she had become the wife of Chaquiweshe and her father, Pucksinwah, had welcomed the muscular young warrior to their family and made his prediction about the child his daughter would bear. The child that would now soon be born. The spasm passed and physical pain dwindled, but the mental anguish became more sharply focused as she lay back and stared upward unseeingly through the faintly smoky air in the wegiwa, thinking again of that second day of the Wind Moon — March — when she and Chaquiweshe had become husband and wife.

The marriage had taken place in the Shawnee village called Kispoko Town far up the Scioto River in the Ohio Country, not many miles upstream from the mouth of Paint Creek. There, on the west bank, was where Tecumapese and four of her five brothers — one older and four younger than she — had been born, across the Scioto from the great fertile basin called the Pickaway Plains. Just as her elder brother, Chiksika — Gunshot — was widely known for his great hunting skills and his remarkable prowess as a warrior, so too was Tecumapese well known because of her beauty and stately bearing, even as a child.

By her fifteenth year she was already taller by inches than her mother, and her long black hair — almost always worn in a single thick braid — shone as if with inner light. Her extraordinarily expressive dark eyes were large, set above high cheekbones that imparted a distinct dignity to her appearance and heightened the delicacy of her other features. Little wonder that her hand was sought by many an admiring young warrior. Of them all, however, it was to her elder brother's best friend, Chaquiweshe, that she was most attracted.

Even though Chaquiweshe — The Mink — was two years older than Chiksika, the two young men had been inseparable friends since they were boys. Both were well built, with swift reflexes and keen intelligence. Together they had learned to hunt and fish and to excel at the games and races participated in by all the young men. Together, eventually, they had become warriors and made outstanding reputations for themselves in the tribe. In the case of Chiksika this was no less than expected. After all, Pucksinwah was his father and there was no greater warrior anywhere. Pucksinwah was not only principal chief of the Kispokotha sept, one of the five social divisions of the tribe, he was war chief of the Shawnees.

And so, just after the Wind Moon had begun, Chaquiweshe and Tecumapese were married — she in her sixteenth year and he in his twentieth. From villages all over the Ohio Country the Shawnees had come to attend the festivities at the marriage of the daughter of their war chief and among them was no less a personage than Hokolesqua, principal chief of all the Shawnees, whose village was at the southern edge of the Pickaway Plains on the bank of Scippo Creek. It was a gala affair, with dancing and games and a great feast of venison and turkey. Chiksika in particular had been enormously pleased at having his best friend become the husband of his sister. And it was during this happy time, while there was laughter and lightness, that Pucksinwah approached the muscular young Chaquiweshe and placed his hand on his shoulder.

"Today you have become a member of our family, Chaqui," Pucksinwah said, using the shortened form of the young man's name for the first time. The war chief smiled. "It is good. We welcome you as a son and brother and husband." He glanced toward his daughter and his expression softened as he looked back at Chaquiweshe and continued. "Before the first deep snow of winter, Tecumapese will bear you a son."

Immediately there were exclamations of pleasure and no one doubted what had been said, for it was well known that Pucksinwah had prophetic ability and what he said would be, would come to pass. It had always been so. Tecumapese had rushed to her father and embraced him and it was perhaps because she was looking at him so closely that she detected a cloaked reserve behind his pleasure, as if he had seen something else ahead beside the birth of his grandson — something much less pleasurable. And though she did not question it, Tecumapese remembered that expression and wondered. Only later did it become all too clear.

Tecumapese and Methotasa had remembered that day together as they waited here in the wegiwa for the birth of the son Pucksinwah had predicted would come and, in discussing it, they had remembered as well the events that had followed. Pucksinwah was, at forty, a very powerful man in his prime, highly intelligent and articulate, and his wegiwa in Kispoko Town had long been a focal point for the collection and dissemination of news which affected the tribe. There were few matters of any consequence that occurred eastward of the great grandmother of rivers, the Missitheepi, of which he was not cognizant, and his grasp of broad trends was incredible and very accurate. And throughout the remainder of spring and summer the trends were very ominous. Hostilities had increased with the white men who penetrated ever deeper into the Indian territory, floating silently downstream on the broad liquid highway they called the Ohio River, but which the Shawnees knew as the Spaylaywitheepi. With no provocation, these intruders rafting downriver had begun shooting the deer and elk, bear and wolves and other game encountered along the shores, not so much as a source of food as simply a form of "amusement," since often the downed animals were left lying where they had fallen. The macabre pastime expanded to include Indians spied along the shores, and soon villages throughout the Ohio country were mourning the loss of husbands, fathers, sons and friends who would never again come home. There had been retaliation, of course, but killing the settlers did not restore the Indians whom the whites had slain.

Then to Pucksinwah's ears came word that the Shemanese — the Long Knives — from Virginia were mounting an army under their colonial governor, Lord Dunmore, to come against the Shawnees. Tecumapese remembered only too clearly the excitement and consternation this news had created. She stirred now, shifting position as the pains of her labor became greater and more frequent, moving into a sitting position on a blanket atop the bison hide, her back against the fur-covered inner wall of the wegiwa, her feet firmly planted and wide apart. Immediately Methotasa was beside her, helping. Still the memories persisted: memories of the large force of warriors gathered by Pucksinwah. She remembered the great war dance that was held and the preparation of weapons — bows and arrows, spears decorated with feathers, tomahawks and war clubs and knives. In her mind's eye she could still see the meticulous way the warriors painted their faces with lines and patterns of white and black and vermilion to strike fear into the hearts of their enemies. And as if it had only been yesterday, she could see them heading away to intercept the army of Shemanese, her father leading the war party, her husband and brother side by side close behind him.

It was on that point of land where the Great Kanawha River flowed into the Spaylaywitheepi from the south that they had encountered the left wing of Lord Dunmore's army under Colonel Andrew Lewis and engaged in a fierce battle on the tenth

day of the Harvest Moon. Seventy-five militiamen were killed,
another one hundred forty-four wounded, as opposed to twenty-
two Shawnees killed and eighteen wounded. Had the fighting
continued it would surely have turned into a disastrous defeat
for the Shemanese, but abruptly the Indians withdrew across
the Spalaywitheepi, their heart for the fight taken away, since
one of those killed was Pucksinwah and another was Chaquiweshe. Two weeks later, only a couple of miles from Kispoko
Town, a treaty of peace was signed on the Pickaway Plains between the Indians and the Shemanese. The Virginians had gone
home and the Indians had returned to their villages; but Chaquiweshe and Pucksinwah were dead.

The son to be born to Tecumapese this day would never know
his father or grandfather. The wegiwa where this birth would
take place was not the one in which Tecumapese and four of her
five brothers had been born, nor was it even in Kispoko Town.
Tecumapese and Methotasa no longer lived among the Kispokotha Shawnees. This was the wegiwa of Chief Black Fish of
the Chalahgawtha Shawnees, situated on the east bank of the
Little Miami River about fifty miles west of Kispoko Town. Both
women were now the wards of Black Fish, peace chief of the
Shawnee nation, in accordance to the Shawnee tradition that
upon the death of a war chief, his family automatically became
wards of the peace chief and moved into his household. Even
Kispoko Town was no longer known by that name; it had become Shemeneto's Town, named after the tribe's new war chief
who had succeeded Pucksinwah there, Chief Shemeneto — Black
Snake. Following the mournful burial ceremonies for those who
had fallen at the Battle of Point Pleasant, Methotasa and her
daughter and five sons had moved here to Chalahgawtha. Black
Fish, who had been Pucksinwah's close friend for many years,
was a wise, honorable and kind peace chief and there was no
doubt he would provide good care for his new wards, but nothing at this point could ease the pain still abiding in the hearts of
Methotasa, Tecumapese and the five sons of Pucksinwah.

Tecumapese made a small sound and then nodded at her mother. It was time for the birth, and immediately Methotasa gave her instructions — the same instructions handed down by Shawnee mothers to their daughters for unnumbered generations. Obeying, Tecumapese squatted with her feet flat to the floor and spread widely apart. As Methotasa helped balance her so she would not fall with her exertions, Tecumapese delivered the baby into her own hands, no sound whatever escaping her. Neither woman remarked on the fact that it was a boy, since neither had doubted for an instant it would be, just as Pucksinwah had predicted.

Although it was not a prerequisite, the naming of a boy born into the Shawnee tribe could be delayed for up to ten days while waiting for something of significance to occur that might suggest an appropriate name. This was the basis for many Indians bearing such names as Barking Dog, Leaning Tree, Black Turkey, Burning Stick and others. In this case, however, there was no need for delay. As long ago as midsummer, Chaquiweshe and Tecumapese had decided what their son would be called. The only thing that might have altered this would have been the occurrence of some truly significant event at the moment of birth or shortly thereafter, indicating that Moneto, highest deity of the Shawnees, had wished otherwise.

The infant boy had made no sound since his birth save for the faintest of whimpers and now lay contentedly in his mother's arms, swaddled in a coverlet of very soft rabbit fur. Since there had been no cries made by either mother or babe, Tecumapese knew that her brothers, waiting outside, were as yet unaware that the baby had been born and so now she raised her voice in a call for them to come in. They entered gravely, Chiksika holding two of the three-year-old triplets, his six-year-old brother holding the third. The six-year-old was a very nice-looking boy and the only one of the five who had not been born in Pucksinwah's wegiwa in Kispoko Town. In fact, he had been born less than a mile northeast of this very spot, at a spring where Pucksinwah and Methotasa had camped when she went into labor during a journey to Chalahgawtha. His name was Tecumseh — The Panther Passing Across — for almost at the very moment of his birth a great comet, which in Shawnee mythology was a panther, had streaked across the night sky. The three-year-olds were already famous in the tribe, for the birth of triplets was an almost unprecedented occurrence among the Shawnees. The two being carried by eighteen-year-old Chiksika were Kumskaka — A-Cat-that-Flies-in-the-Air — and Sauwaseekau — A-Door-Opened. The third, squirming irritably in Tecumseh's arms was, from the moment of his birth, the most vocal of the three and his name was Lowawluwaysica — He-Makes-a-Loud-Noise.

The boys, smiling broadly, stopped at the foot of the bison robe upon which their sister lay propped against the wall and she opened the swaddling to show them the baby. Her answering smile was wan.

"You are now uncles," she told them. "Chiksika, Tecumseh, Kumskaka, Sauwaseekau, Lowawluwaysica — this is your nephew. His name is Spemica Lawba" — Big Horn.

CHAPTER II

October 17, 1786 - Sunrise

N THE VERGE of having completed his twelfth year, Spemica Lawba was a very fine looking young Shawnee. He was tall and lean, with shoulder-length hair every bit as richly glossy black as his mother's, held back from his face by an inch-wide headband of dark red cloth. His coppery-bronze skin was smooth, without blemish, and strong chiseled features were complemented by eyes that were large and dark and very intelligent.

As usual, when deeply engrossed in a project, he was humming softly. They were oddly cadenced tones, sometimes the melodies taught him by Kisahthoi and Tebethto, sometimes the strange rhythmic notes of traditional Shawnee songs and chants taught him by Tecumapese, but most often a peculiar and compelling combination of the two blended in a manner peculiar to Spemica Lawba alone.

His project today as he sat on a blanket close to the central fire of the wegiwa was the construction of a new bow. He had been working on it for more than a week and under his skillful hands it was becoming a beautiful instrument that he knew would serve him well in both hunting and warfare. His raw material was osage wood; osage because of its great resiliency and strength which allowed it to bend smoothly under steady pull to an arc well beyond that at which other woods cracked or snapped. And osage, unlike the limber hickory and ash sometimes used for bowmaking, could be kept strung for long periods of time without taking a set or weakening. Over many weeks he had searched for the ideal piece of osage — a difficult search because osage limbs tended to gnarl as they grew and finding a straight true-grain limb was a significant achievement. When at last he found and cut the proper piece and brought it back to the village it was the cause of much comment and admiration and quite a few of the Shawnee warriors had coveted it, offering to trade good skinning knives or a new British-made tomahawk for the raw material. One had even offered to trade a serviceable flintlock rifle for it and another had offered a fairly good horse — one of several taken on a recent raid against the Kentucky settlements. Though tempted, Spemica Lawba had refused, knowing the value of his find and realizing that if he made his bow well, it would last him for many years, perhaps even a lifetime.

Now, as he continued to scrape its length very carefully with a piece of gray chipped flint, Tecumapese, who was busy moistening finely ground corn flour, kneading it on a flat stone and then shaping it into small round loaves, looked up from her work at him and smiled.

"If you make that wood any smoother, Spemica Lawba," she said, "it will become like the eels that swim up the river each spring; it will slip out of your hand whenever you try to grasp it."

Kisahthoi and Tebethto giggled. The two young women, sitting side by side on a mat, paused in their tasks and waited for Spemica Lawba's reaction. The boy looked at his mother and grinned widely, exposing strong white teeth, with one of his large incisors chipped at the edge. He shook his head. "No, it will cling to me. It knows I am its master. Besides, I am making it into a magical bow. Even if I should lose it, it will be so smooth that it will slide through the grasses like a snake and find its way back to me."

The two sisters clapped their hands and Spemica Lawba swiveled around to look at them in a self-satisfied manner, then dipped his head in mock gravity at their approval. All three women laughed aloud and Spemica Lawba joined them in it. The sound filled the wegiwa and in the midst of it Tecumapese felt a pang, wishing that the men were here and that it could always be this way, as it was in the old times when there was much laughter and lightness. In those days when the men went away it was to hunt, not to engage in warfare with white men. What kind of a world was it, she wondered, in which her son would grow to manhood? Would there be any laughter left at all in any of them, or would conditions continue to degenerate as they had over the past years where loss and destruction and grief reigned, where laughter and lightness and a rich family life constantly diminished? She shook away the thoughts with an effort and spoke to the two younger women.

"Let's get back to our work. We want to get as much done as possible before the call."

The young women nodded and, still smiling, bent back to their tasks. Kisahthoi was cutting and sewing pieces of buckskin into garments, while Tebethto was stringing small apples on long cords to hang them out in the sun to dry for winter's use. The sun was no more than minutes high and the village of Mackachack was still very quiet. Outside a few children could be heard playing their games and some of the women were passing to and from the creek for water or to wash clothing, but the big job of continuing to harvest the corn from extensive fields at the village's perimeter had not yet begun for the day. When the call for that was sounded, as it no doubt soon would be, most of the population would drop whatever they were doing and join together in that community effort.

Continuing to look at the sisters, Tecumapese shook her head slightly. It was hard for her to believe that these two once were white. In the early years just after they had been adopted into the family, the knowledge was always there that they were white, even though the adoption ceremony was said to wash away all white blood and truly make them Indians. But over the years they had become so much imbued with tribal life that Tecumapese actually had all but forgotten their heritage. Still, every now and then one or the other of the sisters would say something or look a certain way and that would trigger a rush of memories . . .

After the Battle of Point Pleasant where her husband and father had been killed, resulting in the loosely formulated treaty made with Lord Dunmore at the Pickaway Plains, the Shawnees had lived up to the letter of the agreement. Hokolesqua had seen to that. "If the treaty is to be broken," had said the Shawnee principal chief whom the whites knew as Cornstalk, "then it will be broken by the white man, not by the Indian." And since Hokolesqua was a very strong leader, his people obeyed. But the increasing influx of white settlers rafting down the Spaylaywitheepi to establish themselves in Kentucky quickly degenerated the principles of the treaty. Whites crossed the river into the Ohio Country to hunt the game the Indians considered theirs, erected cabins on land which they had no right to occupy, and once again began killing Indians indiscriminately wherever encountered. Hokolesqua restrained his people from retaliation as long as he could, but at last the limit was reached. On the third anniversary of the Battle of Point Pleasant he appeared unarmed under a flag of truce at Fort Randolph, which had been built at the battle site. With him had come his son, Elinipsico, and one of his subchiefs, Red Hawk. Hokolesqua had always been a very honorable man and the purpose of the visit was to give fair warning to the fort's commander, Captain Arbuckle, that he could no longer restrain his people from retaliation for the injuries they were receiving. Arbuckle, ignoring the flag of truce, had the three Shawnees thrown into a cell and within an hour a group of soldiers and frontiersmen broke in and shot all three to death in a furious burst of gunfire.

The shock and anger that swept through the Shawnees at the murder of their chief, his son and his subchief were terrible. Vengeance was mandated and frontier warfare again broke out. Black Fish succeeded Hokolesqua as principal chief of the Shawnees, Cornstalk's Town was abandoned and Chalahgawtha became the capital village of the tribe. One of the smaller of the raiding parties to leave Chalahgawtha consisted of only twelve young warriors. It was led by Chiksika, whose second-in-command was his good friend Wasegoboah — Stand Firm. And once again Tecumapese had felt the fear that came with watching her loved ones set off toward possible death, for she loved not only her brother, Chiksika, but also Wasegoboah, whom she felt would one day become her husband and a father to Spemica Lawba.

This time the fears had not been realized. Chiksika and Wasegoboah were gone nearly a month and returned victoriously with considerable plunder, two scalps and two prisoners. The captives were two little girls named McKenzie — Margaret, twelve, and Elizabeth, ten. Margaret had very blond hair, while Elizabeth's was dark. The sisters were adopted by Black Fish, and since Tecumapese and her brothers were also wards of Black Fish, they all became members of the same family. With their adoption, the sisters were renamed — Margaret becoming Matchsquathi Kisahthoi and Elizabeth becoming Matchsquathi Tebethto. The names meant Little Sun and Little Moon. They had adjusted well to tribal life and seemed to relish the work they did along with other members of the family, which included caring for little Spemica Lawba, who was only three and a half at the time of their arrival in Chalahgawtha.

Part of what they had done since becoming members of the family was to teach Tecumseh and Spemica Lawba to speak English, while at the same time learning the Shawnee tongue themselves. Chiksika and Tecumapese had been too busy to learn from the girls and the triplets too disinterested. Tecumseh was an exceptional student and learned from the girls much more swiftly than they from him, and his ability became even more improved when, later, a captive youth his own age, named Stephen Ruddell, was also adopted into the family and renamed Sinnanatha — Big Fish. The boys quickly became friends and made a pact with one another: when together, Tecumseh would speak only English and Sinnanatha would speak only Shawnee. In this way, constantly instructing and correcting one another, both learned very swiftly. Spemica Lawba, being so much younger and learning more from simply overhearing rather than from specific instruction, learned less rapidly. Nevertheless, the little boy learned a great deal of English from them.

During the eight years since Kisahthoi and Tebethto became members of the family, momentous things had occurred among the Shawnees and the whites. The Shemanese declared themselves independent of the British and became engaged in a war of revolution. Since the white settlers of the valley of the Spaylaywitheepi remained at war with the Shawnees, the Indians allied themselves to the British to fight those who called themselves Americans.

When Spemica Lawba was nearly four, one of the most famed of the American frontiersmen was captured and brought to Chalahgawtha. He called himself Simon Butler, although his name was really Simon Kenton. Wide-eyed, Spemica Lawba watched as the captive was forced to run the gauntlet until nearly beaten to death and then saw him forced to undergo various indignities from some of the Shawnee women and children as he lay tied in helpless, spread-eagled position on the ground. Throughout it all the big white man bore his pain and humiliation without complaint and, though much too young to put it into words, Spemica Lawba felt a great admiration for the captive, as well as an overwhelming sympathy . . . and the little Shawnee boy felt a great guilt as well for feeling as he did toward an enemy of his people. Condemned to death by the Shawnees, the frontiersman was taken northward from Chalahgawtha to Wapatomica, the geographical center of the Shawnee nation, to be executed. Instead, he was purchased by the British and taken to Detroit where he was questioned as a spy and imprisoned.

Before he was five, Spemica Lawba witnessed another great sadness among the Shawnees — the splitting of the tribe. For years the elders had argued in their councils about what course to take in light of the continuing encroachment of the whites into their territory. The majority felt there was no way this great white tide could be stopped and that their only safety lay in migrating far to the westward of the grandmother of all rivers, the Missitheepi, trusting that river to be a barrier the whites would not cross. A smaller portion of the tribe, which included Black Fish and his wards, felt that nothing could stop the whites and the only hope lay in remaining where the tribe was now, in its own land, and continuing to make every effort to defend it and drive the whites back. The argument was unresolvable and ultimately, during the Wind Moon — March — of 1779, the tribe split forever. Four thousand Shawnees migrated westward permanently. Although comprised of Shawnees from all five septs of the tribe, the faction that left on that day, led away by its new principal chief, Ki-kusgow-lowa, was made up primarily of members of the Thawegila, Peckuwe and Kispokotha septs. Ki-kusgow-lowa was himself a Thawegila and he was flanked by Chief Yellow Hawk of the Peckuwe sept and Black Stump, the new chief of the Kispokotha. Shemeneto — Black Snake — had stepped down in Black Stump's favor, preferring to remain behind as war chief under Black Fish to lead the less than three thousand who stayed here in the Ohio Country — largely members of the Chalahgawtha and Maykujay septs — with the avowed intention of defending to the death, if need be, their land and dignity.

Late in the spring of that same year, Simon Kenton escaped from Detroit and returned to Kentucky where he reported details heretofore unknown about the location and strength of the Shawnee capital, Chalahgawtha. A military expedition marched

out of Kentucky to attack the Shawnees there. Fortunately, Black
Fish was warned of the impending attack and so he ordered the
village temporarily abandoned. The attackers arrived in July to
find only a deserted town, which they burned and then retreated under fire from a party of warriors led by Black Fish.
Black Fish's hip was shattered by a rifle ball in the fight. Chalahgawtha was rebuilt, but Black Fish's wound failed to heal and
his condition gradually deteriorated until he died the following
October. Chiksika became head of the family, then, and Chief
Catahecassa — Black Hoof — became the new principal chief of
the Shawnees.

To that point there had been little in Spemica Lawba's young
life to bring great cheer, but that was rectified during the next
Planting Moon — May — when his mother and Wasegoboah
were married and he abruptly had a new father. And Wasegoboah — a strong, intelligent, thoughtful man — was indeed a
good father and loved his new young son very much. It was a
happy time, but the happiness was abruptly shattered. During
the following Heat Moon — August — another army of Kentuckians marched against Chalahgawtha. Once again a warning
came to the tribe in ample time for the Shawnee valuables to be
hidden and the town abandoned before the attackers arrived.
And once again, every structure was burned and all the crops
destroyed. The result was a terribly difficult ensuing winter for
the Shawnees, during which many died, but in the following
Rain Moon — April — Chalahgawtha was rebuilt for a third
time.

In August 1782, the Shawnees, aided by British from Detroit,
moved in force against the Kentucky settlements, fought and
won a significant battle against them at a place called Blue Licks,
then retreated accross the Spaylaywitheepi, hoping the whites
had been taught a lesson and would leave the Shawnees alone.
It was not to be. In the following Frost Moon — November —
the Kentuckians marched again and Chalahgawtha was destroyed a fourth and final time. The entire population of Cha-

lahgawtha migrated northward and settled in the scattered Shawnee villages there. That was when Chiksika's family had taken up residence in the new principal village of the tribe — Mackachack. For years this had been the seat of government of the Maykujay sept of the Shawnees and its chief, Moluntha, was the oldest living Shawnee. He was known to have fought against the British in the French and Indian War of 1755 and he was at least a middle-aged man then. He was now, and had been for many years, one of the most respected of all the Shawnee chiefs and believed to have seen at least ninety summers, perhaps more.

Tecumapese sighed aloud, depressed with the chain of thoughts she was experiencing. Would there never again be peace and joy and the simplicity of life that had once been enjoyed by their people?

Kisahthoi glanced up at the sound and her brow furrowed. Almost as if in some inexplicable way she had divined where her adopted sister's thoughts had led her. "Tecumapese?" she said. When Spemica Lawba's mother looked at her expressionlessly, she continued. "Why must the men fight and kill each other? Why can't they just live peacefully with each other and share the fields and woods? Surely there is enough for all."

Tecumapese's smile was wry, and she shrugged. "I often asked the same question when I was younger. Sometimes I still do, but I know now that it can never be: there are too many differences between us which can never be resolved. Many times we have tried to live in peace, but even though treaties were made and hearts were in accord for this goal, it would not work."

"But why not?" Tebethto interjected. "I don't understand why not, if it's what everyone wants."

Tecumapese shook her head, her expression sad. "Our worlds are so different," she said. "You have lived in both, so you should have some idea of it. Look about you. Try to remember what was and what is. The Indian lives with nature, accepting and using with care and restraint and love what Moneto has given to all his children. We do not drive wooden posts into the breast of the Mother earth to divide her into property as the white men do, for we believe the earth belongs to all, to use wisely and well and equally. We hunt in the woods and in the prairies for the animals Moneto has placed there for our needs and we do not take more than we need.

"The whites," she went on, "cut down the forests and burn th⸗ grasses so they can plant things Moneto did not mean to grow here. While they do this, the animals they bring with them are allowed to wander freely and eat the food that belongs to the animals Moneto meant to be here. They kill the deer and elk and often take only the tongue to eat, or perhaps not taking the animals at all, having killed only for some strange gratification they seem to get from killing." She shook her head, unable to comprehend such a thing, then continued softly. "When we allow one white man to build his cabin, soon there are two, then ten and then more until there is little room left. By then the white man has forgotten that the land he is on belongs to the Indians and he has only been allowed to be there as a guest. Suddenly he looks upon the Indian as being an intruder on white man's land and he tells the Indian to move away and make room for more white men who are coming."

Spemica Lawba had stopped polishing his bow and was staring open-mouthed at his mother. He could not remember ever having heard her go on in such a way and had no idea she had ever even given such concepts much thought. She was continuing her comments without pause, a ring of bitterness now in her voice.

"When a white man kills an Indian in a fair fight, it is called honorable; but when an Indian kills a white man in a fair fight it is called murder. When a white army battles Indians and wins, it is called a great victory, but if they lose it is called a massacre and bigger armies are raised. If the Indian flees before the advance of such armies, when he tries to return he finds that white men are living where he had lived. If he tries to fight off such armies, he is killed and the land is taken away. When an Indian is killed it is a great loss which leaves a gap in our people and a sorrow in our heart; when a white is killed, three or four others step up to take his place and there is no end to it. Ever!"

A heavy silence filled the wegiwa following her words. Spemica Lawba glanced at the two sisters and saw that they were staring at Tecumapese in wonder and he knew, as his mother did not, they they could not really sympathize with what she was saying. There was still too much of their white background in them that they kept hidden from her and from Chiksika and Tecumseh and all the others. Only when they were by themselves with Spemica Lawba did they let their own private thoughts become spoken words. Perhaps they thought he was too young to understand the depth of their feelings; perhaps they thought that because they spoke to one another in English he could not very well follow what they were saying, but he knew and understood more than they realized and he was able to sympathize with them, just as he was able to sympathize with his mother. He had heard the two young women talk of their family; of how their father and young brother had been away when the homestead was attacked and of how the war party led by Chiksika had captured the two girls and killed their older brother and their mother. He had heard them speak of their yearnings to one day be reunited with their father and brother, assuming those two were still alive, and he had heard them say on more than one occasion that one day, when the opportunity came, they would simply walk away and rejoin the whites and never come back. What this opportunity would be they could not put into words, but it was something they would recognize when it came. They had been waiting for it ever since their capture eight years ago and they were still waiting for it. Maybe it was just a dream; maybe it would never come. Nevertheless, he knew they were always waiting and he was torn by the feelings within him. In one way he wished they had been able to completely accept their lot, to such extent that they would never wish to return to the white world. On the other hand, he was able to understand their yearning and in quite another way he hoped that the opportunity they sought would one day come to them. If someone had a deep-seated dream that was never entirely absent, shouldn't that person have an opportunity for that dream to come true?

Spemica Lawba was a more than ordinarily sensitive boy, and in his sensitivity he found himself frequently — and often to his confusion and dismay — placing himself in the position of others and wondering how *he* would feel under the same circumstances and what *he* would do if conditions were suitable and he still felt that way. More than once the thought had crossed his mind that when he was old enough and could manage to do so, he would one day take Kisahthoi and Tebethto on horses to where they had been captured and then put them down on their own and tell them to find the lives they had been taken from when they were little girls. He felt he owed them at least this much. And in feeling this way, he often felt great surges of guilt as well, as if he were being unfaithful to his own people. And perhaps he was. Nevertheless, Spemica Lawba, not quite twelve years old, felt very strongly that every person, regardless of who he or she was, had the absolute right to live his or her life as he wished, so long as it did not interfere with the rights of others. And, with the same line of reasoning, he felt very strongly that no person had the right to interfere with the lives of others if those others were not harming him.

Why, he wondered, couldn't things be simple for him, as they seemed to be for others? Why couldn't he accept, without question, the way things were? Why did he experience mental pain from the pain of others and why did he resent those who had power taking advantage of those who had not? He remembered, even as a very little child, how he had silently resented how those contemporaries of his some years ago had taken advantage of the helplessness of a captive frontiersman named Simon Kenton. He remembered how some of the children his own age and older had urinated on the spread-eagled captive or had dug mucus from their noses and spread it on his face and in his eyes and nose and mouth. And he remembered how he had thought it was so wrong for them to act this way and how he had wanted to cry out to them to stop it, to stop what they were doing and act like human beings, not like monsters, and he remembered as well that he had been afraid to open his mouth and express these thoughts, and because of this he was ashamed of himself.

Spemica Lawba looked at his mother and he felt weak with the love he held for her; yet, at the same time, he wondered why she could not see that these two young women who sat here were *captives* who yearned to be free; *prisoners* who wished no one any harm and whose only real desire was to be reunited with their own people. How could anyone, including his own mother, keep such harmless people captive against their will?

In the continuing silence, the boy began quietly scraping his bow again with the piece of chipped flint, feeling with each stroke how the surface of the wood increased in smoothness. Although he was, in a way, comfortable being here with the women and children and old men still remaining in Mackachack, a part of him resented the fact that he was still young enough to be considered a child. He wished he had been old enough to accompany the large war party that had assembled here and left many days ago to join their allies, the warriors of the Potawatomi, Ottawa, Kickapoo and Miami tribes, who were assembling for a great congress on the upper reaches of the Wabash River.

Word of this assembly of the confederacy of tribes had been brought to Kentucky by the spies of the greatly feared George Rogers Clark, who immediately assembled another army of the Shemanese and marched toward the upper Wabash to chastise the Indians for the humiliating defeat suffered at Blue Licks. It was to help their allies in fighting this force of Kentuckians that almost all of the warriors of Mackachack and the other northern Shawnee villages had left. And Spemica Lawba, not quite twelve summers old, was considered still too young to accompany them. He was instructed to remain behind and help with the task of bringing in the vital corn crop while the men were gone. With a disturbing mixture of relief and envy Spemica Lawba had stood with his mother and adopted sisters and watched as the warriors had ridden away from Mackachack, among them his stepfather, Wasegoboah, and his uncles Chiksika, Tecumseh — who was now eighteen — and even the fifteen-year-old triplets, Lowawluwaysica, Kumskaka and Sauwaseekau.

From all outward appearances, Spemica Lawba seemed content and happy as he continued to work on his new osage bow, seeing with satisfaction how the grain became more finely delineated. But even as he worked, his eyes shifted frequently to his adopted sisters, whom he knew better than anyone else. They had cared for him almost as much as his own mother and in those quiet times with them, when Tecumapese and others had not been nearby, they had opened up to him a great deal, telling him what life had been like as a white child and how much they missed that life. And it was they who had, mostly unknowingly, planted in the rich soil of his receptive young mind the seed of belief that there was no reason at all why the Indian and white races could not live together in peace, if only strong efforts were made toward this end, and if the Indians could overcome their own fierce pride. And it was they who, with deliberate subtlety, caused him to feel guilty about the continuing bloodshed on the frontiers, who made him question in his own mind whether it was just not that pride, which they called "misguided," that compelled the Indians to continue in their efforts to drive back the whites. Finally, it was the sisters who caused him to be, deep in the innermost recesses of his heart, almost ashamed of his own heritage.

Kisahthoi, at twenty, had developed into a mature young woman of strong stature, considerably taller than most of the women of Mackachack and with a distinctly athletic build. Her long blond hair was now worn in two queues that fell on either side of her ample breasts, and both she and her sister almost always wore the same sort of clothing she had on now — a simple short-sleeved deerskin pullover garment that fell just below the knee. As usual, her small feet were clad in comfortable moccasins.

Tebethto, darker and shorter than her sister, was more delicate in physique. She, too, wore her hair in long queues, but often tied them behind her or coiled them atop her head. She was still of a more subdued personality than Kisahthoi, but whatever their physical and personality differences, the two remained very close.

They rarely talked — at least where they could be heard by anyone but Spemica Lawba — of the life they had had as the McKenzie sisters on the Kanawha River eight years ago. To Tecumapese and Wasegoboah and the others, it seemed evident that they had forgotten all about their white background and considered themselves to be as much Shawnee as anyone else here and content with their lot. Even Spemica Lawba was almost sure that at this point they had come to the conclusion that one day each would marry a warrior of the tribe and have her own family. But at the same time, the boy knew beyond doubt that Kisahthoi — if not Tebethto as well — still dreamed of her father at intervals and dreamed of being reunited with him; and in these dreams she was still Margaret, and her sister was still Elizabeth.

Abruptly a dog began a furious barking outside the wegiwa and then others joined in until there was quite a din. They could hear voices and a few shouts and for a moment the occupants of the wegiwa stared at one another. Then they leaped to their feet and rushed outside. The same thing was occurring elsewhere, with everyone looking out across a prairie to the south. A lone white man was approaching at trot, holding aloft a dingy white kerchief tied to a stick. Already the few warriors left in the village were moving out to meet him and a sense of tension lay heavy in the air.

The warriors surrounded the arrival and began attempting to question him, but it was quickly obvious that they could not understand him and themselves be understood. In a few minutes one of the warriors, whose name was Anequoi — The Squirrel — came running back toward the village and did not stop until he reached Tecumapese.

"It is one of the Shemanese," he said, the term *Shemanese* in these recent years referring to Kentuckians specifically since the Americans had won their war with the British and were now calling this country the United States. "He has much to say, but we cannot understand. Spemica Lawba," he pointed at the boy, "has learned much of their tongue from Sinnanatha. We need him to come with us and tell us what the man is saying."

Tecumapese nodded, and immediately Spemica Lawba sprinted away with the warrior, leaving Kisathoi and Tebethto, who were basically responsible for the boy's ability to understand English, to wonder why they had not been asked to interpret.

CHAPTER III

October 17, 1786 - Forenoon

PEMICA LAWBA loped beside Anequoi to where the white man was being held by a tall, lean Shawnee named Wapeake — Cold Earth — who, like Anequoi, was one of less than a dozen warriors who had remained behind to guard Mackachack. Some — Anequoi and Wapeake among them — were strong warriors in good condition who had merely been selected to remain behind as a home guard. Most of the warriors on hand, however, apart from an additional half dozen or so who were in their old age, had been kept from going with the expedition to the upper Wabash because of illness or injury.

"I can understand nothing this quaking white quail says," Wapeake told them, punching the man solidly in the side with the handle of his tomahawk. The captive, a gawky, beak-nosed individual with extremely prominent Adam's apple, grunted in pain and cringed. His cheeks were wet with tears which still flowed and he was trembling so badly he could hardly stand.

"What is your name?" Spemica Lawba asked him as sternly as he could. "Why have you come here?"

"Oh, thank the good God A'mighty," the man exclaimed, "you k'n speak English!"

"Answer!" the boy commanded. "Who are you?"

"Chadley. My . . . my name's Willis Chadley. I'm from

25

Kentucky. Lexington. I'm new there. Only two months. I was
with General Logan's army and —"

"What is he saying, Spemica Lawba?" Anequoi demanded,
interrupting. "Interpret as he speaks!"

The youth nodded and told them what Chadley had already
said, then continued with the captive, pausing frequently to interpret for his companions. "Who is this General Logan? Where
is his army now? Where is it going?"

Chadley, still trembling, looked at the two warriors fearfully
and what he saw in their eyes was not encouraging. "Tell 'em
not to hurt me," he implored. "I've come here to help, to warn
about the army comin' here. I'm a friend. They shouldn't hurt
me. They should . . . uh . . . maybe *pay* me for my information. Tell 'em it's damn 'portant and I gotta be paid for it. Risked
my life bringin' it here."

Spemica Lawba interpreted and the expressions of both men
filled with contempt. Cowardice was bad enough; betrayal of
one's own people on top of that was despicable. Wapeake nodded slowly and spoke through tightened lips. "Tell him to speak
and we will pay him well."

The young Shawnee relayed the message and Willis Chadley
relaxed a little, though his fear did not entirely leave. He kept
glancing nervously at the knife and war club in Anequoi's waistband and the tomahawk that Wapeake still held loosely.

"You said the army is coming here?" Spemica Lawba asked.

Chadley nodded. "Yep. General Logan — he was with Clark
as Clark's second-in-command. They was some ways southwest
of here, headin' for the upper Wabash, but then Clark's spies
come in an' tol' him the Maykujay Shawnee warriors had left
these villages," — he made a sweeping motion with one hand,
indicating Mackachack — "to join the Wabash confederacy and
he figgered he had to do somethin' to draw 'em back to the Maykujay towns. He sent Logan back to Kentucky to raise more
men and march against the towns while Clark and his army
pushed on toward the Wabash. So Logan, he came back and

sent out a call for volunteers an' in no time he got almost eight hundred. That's who's coming."

"You were part of that army?" Spemica Lawba asked the question after interpreting for Anequoi and Wapeake, whose eyes narrowed.

Chadley nodded. "A private."

"And you deserted from the army to come here?"

"Yep. I ain't got hardly nothin' back in Kentucky an' I figgered the Injens'd be so grateful for me warning 'em that they'd give me somethin'; mebbe some of that there silver ever'one says you got."

Spemica Lawba and the warriors conversed briefly and then the questioning continued. "Where was the army when you left it? When did you leave?"

"We was camped on Todd's Fork. At least the creek we call Todd's Fork. South of here, mebbe sixty miles. Left 'em right after dark night 'fore last an' I ain't hardly stopped. Reckon they figure I lit out for Kentucky. Well, I ain't going back there. I'm wore out an' hungry. Been eatin' nothin' but parched corn and johnny-cake. You got something to feed me? Then you can give me my pay for the warnin' an' I'll be on my way. You won't see me no more. I'm leavin' this country."

As Spemica Lawba interpreted these remarks, Wapeake moved surreptitiously behind Chadley, out of the white man's line of vision. As the young Shawnee finished, Wapeake's arm moved unexpectedly in a flashing arc and he buried his tomahawk to the hilt in Chadley's head. With a small expulsion of breath, the Kentuckian fell to the ground, his limbs moving spastically for a moment, and then all movement ceased. Wapeake jerked his tomahawk free, scalped the man swiftly and came to his feet.

"There is his reward," he grated. "It is the only pay any traitor should receive." He shook excess blood from the scalp and then added, "Come. We have to tell Moluntha."

Spemica Lawba was staring, having been as unprepared as Chadley for what occurred. Now, as the two warriors loped off toward the village, he glanced one more time at the body of Chadley and then raced after them. The three reached the large wegiwa of Chief Moluntha simultaneously. The old chief, his long gray hair dingy yellowish with age and hanging loosely to his shoulders, was standing expressionlessly at the doorway as they came to a halt before him. Another young warrior with an injured arm stood beside him and two old men, though these latter two were nowhere near so old as Moluntha. Several women and a few children had also gathered in a little cluster nearby and were watching fearfully.

Anequoi reported quickly to him what Spemica Lawba's interpretation had been of Chadley's remarks and grave concern came into the chief's lined old face. He placed a hand on Spemica Lawba's shoulder and said, "You see, my son, those who stay behind can be of value, too. You have done well." The youth felt the leap of pride in his breast and he grinned. Moluntha turned to the others, addressing them all. "Since that man . . ." his eyes flicked momentarily toward where the distant body of Chadley still lay, ". . . deserted the Shemanese two evenings ago and came directly, evidently as rapidly as he could, the army of the Shemanese, which undoubtedly will move more slowly, cannot possibly arrive here before tomorrow, since they would not have discovered his absence until the morning after he left. And as he said, they probably believe he took the coward's path and fled back to safety across the Spaylaywitheepi. But we will take no chances. Spread the word to all those who remain here: we must gather up those goods we should not leave behind and abandon Mackachack before today's sun is straight up. Go!"

The warriors turned and raced off, lifting their voices as they ran, relaying the orders of their chief. Spemica Lawba, still uplifted with Moluntha's praise of him, ran directly to his wegiwa and babbled a breathless explanation of what had transpired, adding, concerning Chadley, "He was a bad man. He wanted silver from us for betraying his own people. He was very bad."

They quickly set about gathering up those items that it was important for them to take — not only their own personal items, but those belonging to Wasegoboah and Chiksika as well as Tecumseh and the triplets — and tying them into bundles made from blankets and fur skins. They took medicine bags and cosmetics, jewelry — mostly silver arm- and legbands and necklaces — and packets of shelled corn, meal, sugar and other foodstuffs, extra moccasins and garments, smaller gardening tools, strings of wampum and loose wampum beads in little pouches. They took small personal treasures of their own, worthless to anyone else but which almost certainly would be destroyed or taken if left behind. And they took weapons. Spemica Lawba carefully stowed away the nearly completed osage bow and attached his tomahawk and sheathed skinning knife firmly in the waistband of his leggins. The knife was especially treasured by him — an excellent knife, sharply pointed and kept honed to a razor's edge, its haft fashioned of walnut and beautifully overlaid with a long, spiraling half-inch-wide ribbon of finest buckskin that had first been soaked and stretched, then wrapped firmly about the haft and allowed to dry. It had been a gift to him from his stepfather, Wasegoboah.

They worked quickly and without unnecessary conversation and their work was nearly finished two hours before the sun was at its zenith. Everyone else, it seemed, had worked with equal swiftness and it appeared they would be able to move away from the town well in advance of the deadline Moluntha had set. But wise as he had been in ordering swift action, old Moluntha had miscalculated in one very important respect. Because the deserter, Chadley, had arrived on foot, he had assumed the entire advancing army was afoot as well. Not only were they mounted, Benjamin Logan moved them with a speed little short of phenomenal, following the trail of Willis Chadley. The American commander might not have been able to do this so well had he not had, as his chief scout and guide, perhaps the greatest tracker among all the frontiersmen, a giant of a man whom the Shawnees knew only too well — Simon Kenton. It was said that

Kenton could track an unshod pony across limestone rock with ease and following Chadley's trail, even though the deserter had attempted to hide it, had been child's play for him. But it hadn't been necessary to track the man far. The spoor Chadley left soon intercepted an Indian path and this trail having been followed by the deserter made it abundantly clear to Kenton where he was heading. Years ago, during his captivity and after having been marched northward out of Chalahgawtha toward his supposed execution, Kenton had been forced to run another gauntlet when they reached Mackachack and he knew the location of the principal Maykujay village very well. And he remembered as well the unexpected kindness he had received from the ancient chief of the Maykujays, Moluntha. Kenton, upon determining where the deserter was heading, had wheeled out immediately and returned to the army, reported his findings to Logan and immediately the commander set his men into a forced march.

Now, at 10 A.M., the army of General Logan broke from cover in three wings and galloped to the attack with fearsome shrieks, brandishing rifles and swords. Almost no resistance was occurring. A few scattered shots were sounding from here and there and a few warriors — Anequoi and Wapeake among them — were making courageous stands against overwhelming odds, not in an effort to win but in the desperate hope of holding back the army just long enough for the women and children to escape. As for the latter, they fled screaming from their wegiwas, scattering as if they were covies of quail bursting from cover.

As the unexpected charge began, Spemica Lawba dropped a large bundle he was taking outside and leaped out the door, racing toward where Chief Moluntha's wegiwa was located, intent on helping the ancient leader if he could. Tecumapese, shrieking his name, ran out of the wegiwa after him but he had already disappeared from her view and she plunged into the heavy cover near the creek bank. Kisahthoi and Tebethto also found their legs and, hand in hand, fled as swiftly as they had ever run, managing to reach the cover of a nearby island of woods without being seen. From hiding they watched in horror what was happening.

In Mackachack itself, the weak resistance was quickly overcome by the attackers. Anequoi was killed with a lead ball through his heart and Wapeake did not last much longer, dying beneath the sword thrust of one of the Kentuckians. Others were also killed during this initial onslaught, including some of the women who held their ground and tried to fight. Most were cut down easily by slashing swords.

Colonel Thomas Kennedy, leading the right wing, spurred his horse after a group of eight squaws fleeing in a cluster, his finely honed Scotch broadsword held high. As he overtook a heavyset middle-aged woman named Sathea, he swung his sword in a savage chop and all but clove her skull in two, nearly losing his sword as she collapsed. Bracing his boot against her head, he jerked the blade free, regained his balance, and then charged after the seven who were still running. In succession he struck down six of them, including a seventeen-year-old named Tima, who had just married the young warrior named Petoui three days before he had ridden out with the war party for the upper Wabash. The final woman, Karalo, wife of a subchief named Red Horse, jerked to a stop, whirled about and tried to surrender, but it was too late. Kennedy was already swinging his sword. She held up a hand to fend off the blow and lost four fingers of that hand as well as suffering a gash on her scalp, but she was still alive. All about, other groups of fleeing squaws and children stopped and fell to their knees crying "*Mat-tah tshi! Mat-tah tshi!*"— Do not kill us!

Kisahthoi and Tebethto, watching from hiding in the woodland, shuddered. Tebethto was weeping silently, almost uncontrollably, but Kisahthoi shook her shoulders fiercely until the eighteen-year-old gained better hold of herself, though still breathing raggedly.

"Listen to me, 'Liz'beth," the elder sister whispered urgently.

It was the first time in a long while that she had addressed her sister by her true name. "We always thought a time would come when we could just walk away."

"And now it's come, Margie," snuffled the dark-haired girl, completing the comment and saying Margaret's nickname with a hard *g*. "What do we do now?"

"We try to get to safety, that's what."

"We could surrender to the soldiers," Elizabeth McKenzie pointed out. "They're white like us."

Margaret McKenzie shook her head. "We're *not* white, 'Liz'beth. We haven't been for years. We've been Shawnees. That's how they would see us and they'd probably kill us just like they did Sathea and Tima and the others." She shook her head again. "No, we've got to head north, not south. Toward where Detroit is. We can get there if we just keep heading that way. We'll start after dark. Right now we've got to hide. Let's go."

She took her younger sister's hand and led her through the woods toward its north edge. Far to their left was one of the village's large cornfields. Straight ahead, just beyond a deep erosion gully, stretched a wide prairie where it was obvious they'd be seen. At Margaret's directions, they moved to the gully and climbed down over the edge, then wedged themselves well out of sight beneath an overhang of earth bound together by the interlaced roots of prairie grasses. As of this moment, the two adopted Shawnee women known as Kisahthoi and Tebethto ceased to exist.

The raiders had swept into the village of Mackachack with such surprise and speed that Spemica Lawba was unable to reach Chief Moluntha's wegiwa before they were virtually upon him. At the last possible instant before being detected, the youth slipped out of sight into the open doorway of the wegiwa next to Moluntha's in the center of Mackachack. A horseman galloped past and almost at the same time he heard the voice of Moluntha shouting *"Bahd-ler! Bahd-ler!"* He realized the horseman was the great Shemanese warrior who had once been a prisoner of the Shawnees, Simon Butler — actually Simon Kenton — whom the Indians had always called Bahd-ler. Moluntha was surrendering! Identifying himself to the huge frontiersman, he extended his tomahawk, haft-first, and offered to surrender himself and his three wives, who clustered behind him, to Bahd-ler. The frontiersman leaned down and accepted Moluntha's tomahawk as a group of eight privates galloped up and came to a halt.

"The chief and his wives have surrendered," he told them. "You men form a protective ring around them while I go fetch Ben Logan."

The horsemen did as ordered and Kenton thundered off, while Moluntha and his wives, he far more calm than they, stood quietly waiting. Although most Shawnees in these days practiced monogamy, some of the older chiefs of the tribe still remained polygamous, as most of the Shawnee men had been many years ago. Moluntha had had five wives simultaneously but he had already outlived two of them. In less than two minutes Kenton was back with Logan, who was mounted on a fine chestnut mare. The general was a fine-looking man with kindly eyes, a broad forehead and strong jaw. Though only of medium height, his was a commanding figure, giving the impression of being much larger than he actually was. He rode with skill and, as the two men dismounted, carried himself with a fluid grace that bespoke powerful reserves of energy. The circle of privates opened to give them admittance. Moluntha smiled toothlessly and extended his arm in greeting. Both Kenton and Logan shook the skeletal hand. Then the Shawnee chief addressed them in creditable English.

"Moluntha surrenders himself and his wives into the hands of the great white chief, Logan."

From his hiding place, Spemica Lawba saw the commander of the Shemanese smile and nod. "You will not be harmed," the general said. "Nor will your wives." He reached into an inner pocket and removed a piece of paper upon which he swiftly wrote an official protection order. This he handed to Moluntha and then questioned him briefly, in a kindly manner.

Moluntha spoke quietly. "Almost all of our villages are, at this time, like Mackachack, peopled mostly by women and children only, the warriors having gone to fight Clark on the Wabash. This includes Blue Jacket's Town, Girty's Town, Wapatomica and others."

It was what Logan had anticipated and he nodded, then turned and spoke an order to the privates. "You men dismount and keep the protective ring around Chief Moluntha and his wives. You are to hold them as prisoners, but they are not to be harmed in any way. We'll return shortly. Kenton, come with me."

The general and the frontiersmen remounted and rode off as the privates encircled the captives. Hardly a minute later, the initial sound and fury of the attack dwindling, three men rode up and dismounted. Their leader was Captain Hugh McGary. The other two were privates — Ignatius Ross, a bushy-browed, stocky little man, and William Lytle, a man of slightly more than medium height, whose left cheek was etched with a thin pink scar.

"I want to talk to that Indian," McGary said.

"We're under orders to protect him," one of the privates answered.

"By God," the officer thundered, "I'm *Captain* McGary and I intend questioning this man." He pulled a tomahawk from his belt and held it menacingly. "Now let me through or I'll drop any man who stands in my way!"

"I . . . guess it'd be all right if you just questioned him, sir," the spokesman for the privates said. "But you'll have to put that weapon away."

McGary stared at him coldly for a moment and then begrudgingly thrust the haft of the tomahawk back into his belt. "Well?" he grated.

With some hesitation and nervous glances at one another, the privates allowed a gap to form in their lines and McGary strode through, followed by his two companions. The guard of privates moved away more until they were in a loose group rather than the protective ring.

"Who are you?" McGary demanded of the old Shawnee.

Moluntha exhibited no fear. "I am Moluntha," he said. "Chief of the Maykujays. I and my wives have been given a protection by your general." He extended the paper Logan had given him.

McGary ignored the paper. His voice, when he spoke again, was a raspy growl. "Were you at Blue Licks?"

Moluntha did not answer immediately, but his eyes lighted with a small fire and the tiniest trace of a smile tilted his mouth corners. The Blue Licks Battle was the last action Moluntha had seen and he had known at the time that it would be the last expedition in which he would ever participate. Much as he hated to admit it, even to himself — since for decades he had been one of the most legendary fighters among the Shawnees — he knew at Blue Licks that he was just too old to go along with any more war parties against the Kentuckians. But the victory won by the Shawnees at Blue Licks would live in his heart and mind for so long as he lived.

"*Answer me!* Were you at Blue Licks?"

"I was," said Moluntha, drawing himself up to his full height.

"God damn you!" McGary snarled. "I'll give you Blue Licks pay!"

Before anyone could move to stop him, the captain jerked the tomahawk from his belt and buried it in the old man's head in a tremendous blow. Moluntha was killed instantly and slumped to the ground, the official protection paper still clenched in his hand. Even as he was falling his wives had begun shrieking.

Two things happened simultaneously as Moluntha's body collapsed: General Logan galloped up, his expression fierce with barely contained anger, having witnessed the final moments of the tragedy from a short distance away; and Spemica Lawba, tomahawk in hand, burst from the nearby wegiwa doorway with a harsh cry of fury, racing to attack McGary. Some of the privates of the protective guard, initially taken by surprise, were already leaping on the captain and struggling to restrain him. Spemica Lawba's progress was impeded by Ross, who snatched the boy around the waist as he passed. The private hardly anticipated what happened next. With surprising agility and strength, Spemica Lawba wrenched himself out of the man's grip, spun and swung his own tomahawk in a vicious arc. So extremely close was the blow that Ross felt the sharp edge shave away one of his eyebrows without breaking the skin. The private jerked back violently, stumbled and fell on his back. Instantly Spemica Lawba launched himself onto the man, landing with bent knees in his solar plexus, driving out Ross's wind with a great whoosh. Pinning the gasping private's arms with his knees, the Shawnee boy raised his tomahawk again for the final blow. All this happened with such incredible swiftness as to be stunning. Only Private Lytle's quick reaction — snatching the boy's wrist — saved the life of his friend. William Lytle jerked the boy away savagely, yanking the tomahawk out of his hand at the same time. The youth spun, fell, rolled over, and was back on his feet in a crouch, knife in hand, all in one movement.

By this time the others had shaken off their paralysis of surprise and two more of the privates grasped the boy's arms and held him. He continued struggling violently, kicking toward their groins, biting toward their hands, butting with his head. The treasured knife was still in his hand.

General Logan dismounted and walked toward the private, stopping in front of him. "Release him," he said. The two privates looked at one another uncertainly and Logan's nostrils flared. "I said *release him!*"

They let go of his arms and immediately Spemica Lawba was back in his crouch, knife held menacingly. Benjamin Logan was watching him closely and then, surprisingly, he held out his hand, palm up. "Son," he said softly, "I don't know if you can understand the words, but I hope you'll understand the meaning." He smiled genuinely. "Let me have the knife."

The boy stared at him unflinchingly for a long moment and then straightened from his crouch. He dipped his head in acquiescence, flipped the knife so the blade was in his hand, and then placed the haft in Logan's palm. The general's smile widened and now it was he who dipped his head toward the boy. "Thank you. Please wait here."

He turned, strode a few steps to where Captain McGary was being held and addressed him with cold fury. "You are a disgrace!" he said. "You have deliberately disobeyed the orders of your general and what you have done is no less than calculated murder. You are under arrest, sir, and you will remain so until we return to Kentucky, at which time a court-martial will be convened to try you on charges that I myself will bring against you." His gaze shifted to the two soldiers restraining him. "You two men," he said, "are, as of this moment and until I release you from the duty, guards over Mister McGary. You will guard him twenty-four hours a day, preventing his escape. Should he escape," he added darkly, "I shall order you shot." The general turned away, ignoring the naked hatred on the face of McGary. He returned to Spemica Lawba, placed him in the care of two other privates. "Guard him and care for him," he told them. "Should he come to any harm, you will answer to me personally and the consequences will not be pleasant."

He placed his hand on Spemica Lawba's shoulder and his voice gentled. "I trust you will not try to escape. I assure you, no one will harm you. I will get back to you as soon as possible."

The battle, meanwhile, if such it could be called, had ended and captives were rounded up. Twenty-two Indians had been killed, ten of them warriors, the remainder squaws and old men. No children had been killed, although two, along with several women, had been slightly wounded. Three of Logan's soldiers were dead. The general ordered the dead Indians buried in a common grave. The three privates who had been killed were to be buried with prayers and military honors in individual graves dug beside one another in the shade of a large oak.

Thirty-three prisoners were brought together, mainly women

and a few children. Obviously, many times that number had escaped as the attack broke out, Tecumapese among them, but no immediate effort was made to pursue them. The McKenzie girls, who for so many years had been known as Kisahthoi and Tebethto, were discovered by a young British trader, John Kinzie, and escorted to Detroit. General Logan ordered that thirty-two of the prisoners be returned with the army to Danville, there to be held captive for possible prisoner exchange at some future date, as there had been in the past. The single exception was the boy, Spemica Lawba, whom the general retained under his own special protection.

The remainder of the campaign was carried out wholly without resistance. Those who had escaped from Mackachack had swiftly spread out to the other towns, warning them, so all were quickly abandoned. Logan reassembled his army and sent out detachments to a dozen other nearby Shawnee towns, with orders to collect all worthwhile plunder, destroy all the crops, and burn all the villages. This was accomplished in good order and without opposition. In addition to Mackachack, where every wegiwa was burned — including the one containing Spemica Lawba's cherished and nearly completed osage bow — the villages destroyed were Moluntha's Town, Mingo Town, Wapatomica, Mamacomink, Kispoko (also called Girty's Town), Puckshanoses, McKee's Town, Waccachalla, Pecowick, Buckangehela's Town, Blue Jacket's Town and the newest one, another village named Chalahgawtha. Hundreds of acres of corn were destroyed and the total plunder, with a valuation of $2,200, was divided equally among Logan's men.

Before the army set out for its return to Kentucky, Benjamin Logan took young Spemica Lawba aside. He indicated the boy should sit on a log and then sat beside him. In silence the general packed his pipe with tobacco, lighted it, and puffed for a short while. Spemica Lawba watched him closely, masking all expression. At last the man spoke.

"Son," he said, "I have a strong feeling you speak English. Is that correct?"

For a long moment Spemica Lawba did not reply, unwilling to admit to too much, yet somehow trusting this man. At last he nodded and answered, deliberately using broken phraseology. "Speak some," he said. "Understand more."

"Good. You're a very brave lad. I would like to help you. Since you are now a prisoner, you must remain with us. You have a choice, however. You may go with them," he inclined his head toward the assembled prisoners some distance away, "and share whatever their lot will be. Or, if you wish to do so, you may remain with me and I will take care of you."

Again Spemica Lawba did not reply immediately and the silence stretched out for so long a time that Ben Logan finally added, "Did you understand what I said?"

The boy gave up all pretenses and answered directly. "Yes, I understood. I will go with you."

"Excellent." Logan smiled broadly. "I would like very much to adopt you and teach you about your new life. You will be my son. Just as it is the custom among your people to adopt certain captives and give them Shawnee names, so I will adopt you and give you an English name."

A flicker of interest came into the boy's eyes. "What name?"

"What is your name now?" Logan countered.

"Spemica Lawba."

"Which means?"

"Big Horn."

The Kentucky general nodded and sucked on his pipestem a few times. Little clouds of the blue-white tobacco smoke drifted up and away. "From now on," he said at length, "as a member of my family, you will be known by the name of Johnny Logan."

"John-ny Logan." The boy savored the name on his tongue. Then he smiled.

CHAPTER IV

March 10, 1787

JOHNNY LOGAN — for that was how Spemica Lawba thought of himself these days — had never before felt so confused, so torn within himself. He was well into his thirteenth year now and had lived with the Logan family a long time. He had adapted to it extremely well, wore the clothing of the whites, attended school with Kentucky youngsters his own age, and absorbed his new culture with the thirst of a sponge.

The boy seemed to have grown inches in this time, but that physical growth was small as compared to his growth mentally. With phenomenal speed, during this period that he lived with the Logan family, he had learned to read and write, and he devoured books with a speed and retention rarely witnessed. The life he had lived as a Shawnee was still important to him and he held a fierce pride in his heritage, yet he had become so imbued with his new life — had been so warmly and completely accepted by the whole Logan family as son and brother — that now, had he been given the option, there was no doubt whatever that he would have selected life as a white man over that as an Indian. He had learned their ways, eaten at their table, slept in fine soft beds beneath their roof, polished his English to almost flawless fluency, and had been introduced to a great variety of subjects he previously had not known. He learned, with amazement, of the breadth and scope of the civilized world; learned of the great civilizations that had come and gone — Babylonian, Egyptian, Chinese, Greek, Roman — and those which presently existed in France, Spain, England and elsewhere. He learned of such subjects as chemistry and geography, history and mathematics, literature and poetry and art, and he had become all but overwhelmed at the wonder of it all. For the first time he had come to realize how severely limited Indian life was. It was beautiful, true, in its simplicity and closeness to nature, but having now experienced the variety and seemingly endless horizons of a more advanced culture, he wondered privately — and often guilt-ridden at his feelings — how he could ever have been satisfied before Benjamin Logan had adopted him.

Within the fertile soil of Johnny Logan's mind was growing the germ of an idea: a strengthening belief that there was no reason why the Shawnees and other tribes should continue to oppose the whites. There was, he felt, so very much to be gained by melding themselves to the white culture as he had done. What a wonderful thing it would be for his people — for all Indians! — not only to have the proud heritage of their own Indian background, but equally the benefits of the much more advanced culture of the whites, with all the marvelous goods, benefits, comforts, advantages and ideas it had to offer, along with its exciting promise of limitless opportunity.

The youth had become sure that he would remain among the whites for the rest of his life, perhaps returning on occasion to his people to visit friends and relatives. He dreamed that perhaps also, at such times, he would be able to convince others to return with him, to end their futile resistance which in the end, he was convinced, would only lead to their destruction. Certainly concessions would have to be made, compromises by both whites and Indians, for such an assimilation of cultures to occur, but in his youthful optimism he was sure there was no reason why such a dream could not become reality. His eyes glowed and his heart raced as he thought of how much greater value he might be to his people to strive to bring them toward this goal than to serve as a warrior whose sole purpose would be to use weapons to attempt to hold back an uncheckable tide. For one who was only in his thirteenth year, these were indeed weighty matters to be considering, but the kindness and generosity of Benjamin Logan to a young Shawnee named Spemica Lawba had ignited a fire in the youth that could never be extinguished.

Now, though his great desire to see an amalgamation of the white and Indian cultures to the benefit of both remained undiminished, the likelihood of his being a motivating force toward that goal was sharply diminished. On this day he sat silently, morosely, in a boat filled with other Shawnees, mostly women, en route to be returned to his life as an Indian. He and they were being rowed across the Spaylaywitheepi — which now he thought of as the Ohio River — from the Kentucky settlement the whites called Limestone to a point almost directly across on the north bank of the river. It was a day the young Shawnee-turned-white had never envisioned would really come; a day for which he was wholly unprepared.

This was the day of the prisoner exchange.

Johnny Logan was filled with a mixture of emotions — resentment, sorrow, fear, grief, a sense of overwhelming loss and a frustrated anger at the unfairness of it all. He had to keep reminding himself that he was going back to his own people, back to his true family. But he was not a prisoner! Why must he return? Why were not his own desires — particularly his burning desire to stay — taken into consideration? Why could he not, as he so deeply wished, stay here another year or two or even more and go back to the Shawnees only when it was his own decision to go back? In feeling this way, he also experienced a resurgence of the sense of guilt that had plagued him at intervals. He knew he should be overjoyed to be returning to his mother and Wasegoboah, to his uncles and friends and acquaintances. In a way, he *was* overjoyed and eager to be reunited with them, but at the same time he was deeply saddened at being forced to leave the Logan family.

Arrangements for the prisoner exchange had taken many weeks and had been continually hampered by the mutual distrust of the two factions, but eventually the day — *this* day — had been set for that event. On hand for the whites, in addition to Benjamin Logan, who was in charge, were such notable men on this frontier as Simon Kenton, Daniel Boone, Luther Calvin, Robert Todd, George Hany, Ben Whiteman and Robert Patterson, along with more than two score others. In charge of the Indians was Weh-yeh-pih-ehr-sehn-wah, better known to the whites as Blue Jacket, and with him were Black Snake, Captain Billy, Me-ou-se-ka, Wolf, Petowah, King John and some sixty warriors. There was extreme wariness and suspicion on both sides.

More than an hour ago the white leaders had crossed the river to negotiate with the Indians about the impending exchange. The Indian prisoners of the whites, Johnny Logan reluctantly among them, had been held under guard in a cluster on the south shore of the river, awaiting the sign to be given for them to come across when negotiations were concluded. Similarly, the white prisoners of the Indians had been held under guard at a place far back in the woods, awaiting the arrival of the runner who would tell them to advance to the exchange site. And at last the official talking was concluded, red hands joined with white sealing promises of friendship and an end to the hostilities between them — which few present really believed — and then the signal was given. And now, crossing the river, Johnny Logan realized that he would be seeing his adopted father again in a few minutes, for what might be the last time they would ever meet. He was all but engulfed in the sorrow that swelled in him.

The boats scraped ashore and the Indian prisoners disembarked at just about the same time that the white prisoners came into view from the woods. The two groups stood silently a dozen yards apart for a long moment and then the exchange began. There were cries of recognition and joyous reunions, and tears of both gladness and grief. The son of an old German settler, John Kinsaulla, greeted his father, who had been captured a year ago. The younger man wept aloud and told his father that Mrs. Kinsaulla was waiting and praying across the river. A sixteen-year-old white girl, her expression gradually changing from excited anticipation to confused fear, searched in vain among the assembled whites for a member of her family, not yet knowing they had been killed during an Indian raid only weeks after her capture three years before. Major George Hany's two sons, aged thirteen and ten, rushed into his arms and their reunion was extremely emotional. A white woman settler was brought across the river to possibly identify a girl of about nine as hers. The woman's daughter had been taken when still only a toddler, but that child had had a small triangular scar on her forehead at the hairline. The scar was there and the woman shrieked in delight and enfolded the girl in her arms, but the girl also cried out, wrenched herself from the woman's grip and fled screaming "*Nik-yah! Nik-yah!*"— Mother! Mother! — to the squaw who had raised her as her own, begging the Shawnee woman not to give her up. And at last the Shawnee woman, blinded by tears, had covered her ears and stumbled off into the woods as the crying child was taken by the hand and led off by her bewildered blood mother. And there were those on both sides who looked for husbands or wives or children among the captives, but the loved ones were not there and they were stricken with sorrow.

Among the more poignant of the partings was that of Johnny Logan from Benjamin Logan. The two walked off to one side, the man's arm around the youth's shoulders in a warm grip. They stopped beside the trunk of a massive shagbark hickory and simply stood silently together for a considerable time. When the man spoke, his voice was husky with emotion.

"Johnny, we love you very much. I hope you know that. In losing you today, Mrs. Logan and I are losing a son. I know you want to stay, just as we want you to. I wish you could, but the terms of the treaty exchange require that all Indians be given up by us, just as all whites must be given up by the Shawnees. But we won't forget you and we hope in better times we will see you again. This is your home, always. You may come any time you wish and stay for however long you wish."

The eyes of the boy who was both Johnny Logan and Spemica Lawba filled with tears, and he prayed they would not spill over his eyelids and trickle down his cheeks. It was some time before he felt he was enough in control of himself to respond. At last he said, "I love you, too. I will not — could not! — forget you, ever. Now I am supposed to become Spemica Lawba again, and to the Shawnees that is who I will be. But to you and your family, to whatever white people I have any contact with in the future, I will be Johnny Logan. I am becoming a Shawnee again, but no matter what happens between our people, I will never harm you in any way. That is my promise."

Ben Logan nodded and reached into the pouch that was slung to his side. From it he extracted a knife which he handed to the boy, saying, "This belongs to you." It was the same weapon that Spemica Lawba had surrendered to Logan so long ago at Mackachack: the beautifully made knife that had been a gift from his stepfather, Wasegoboah.

The youth looked at it for an extended time and then slowly slid it into his belt. His lower lip was trembling as he looked up at the man. They embraced then and neither could any longer check the tears. When they pulled apart, the youth took the big man's hand in both of his. "To my white father," he reiterated, "I will always be Johnny Logan, and I make this solemn vow to you now: I will never raise my hand against you or your army."

He turned and strode away, head erect, toward where the Indians were clustered preparatory to departure. And as he walked he considered the vow he had just made and he prayed to Moneto that the time would never come when his opposing loyalties would be put to the test.

CHAPTER V

August 20, 1790

HERE WERE those among the Shawnees who declared
darkly that Chiksika and Tecumseh, who had been gone
for over three years, would never be seen again, but
their sister, Tecumapese, did not believe this, nor did her son,
Spemica Lawba. It was therefore a very special day today when
Spemica Lawba was the first to see the man approaching from
the distance and the first to realize who he was.

"Tecumseh! It's *Tecumseh!*" he shouted, alerting the village.
"Tecumseh has come home again!"

It was the most excitement any of them had seen Spemica
Lawba exhibit in the three and a half years since his return to
the Shawnees from captivity.

The young man had changed a great deal during that captivity, however benevolent he claimed it to have been and however
strong his gratitude to the Shemanese general, Benjamin Logan.
Spemica Lawba's reunion with Tecumapese in Wapatomica,
which had become the Shawnee capital following the destruction of Mackachack, had been a wonderfully joyous occasion,
especially since neither mother nor son knew during that long
separation whether the other was still alive. But the changes in
the youth were immediately obvious and became more so as time
passed. He had become very serious of nature, no longer so light

and carefree as he had always been before, and he was given to long periods of thinking deeply, at which times he resented interruptions. Had it been known that what filled his mind was an almost constant effort to think of some way to help draw the Shawnees and Americans to come together in friendship and alliance, he would have been told to concern himself with better things, such as becoming a great hunter, trapper, fisherman and warrior. But they didn't know, and most often they agreed with the prevailing belief that he acted as he did because he very greatly missed his uncles, Chiksika and Tecumseh.

In a way, this was true. His triplet uncles Sauwaseekau, Lowawluwaysica and Kumskaka — only three years his senior, were still close by, of course — but both Sauwaseekau and Kumskaka had gotten married and had families of their own now, and Lowawluwaysica had become very strange. Some attributed this to the fact that he had lost his right eye to an arrow that accidentally struck him during the games several years ago — an arrow shot by Sauwaseekau — but others contended that he would have been strange in any event. Whatever the case, he was a surly, high-strung, young man with distinctly unappealing features — his ugliness intensified by the empty eyesocket. He boasted much without any basis for his claims. He was prideful and arrogant, bullying toward those who let him get away with it and insincerely fawning to those who would not allow themselves to be bullied. Even as a child, Spemica Lawba had never cared for Lowawluwaysica very much and that feeling had deepened over the years. The two had only one thing in common: a love for Tecumseh that bordered on adoration.

For a long time during the absence of Chiksika and Tecumseh, the Shawnees had heard nothing of them. Then, bits of information had begun filtering in, slowly at first, but then with greater frequency. Visitors from other tribes, especially those to the south, spoke in increasingly glowing terms of the Shawnee brothers who had come to visit them and who had stayed to help them in their struggles against encroaching whites. Tecumseh, they said, had become a phenomenal warrior, renowned for his extreme courage, his coolness in battle, his leadership capabilities and his remarkable combination of almost total fearlessness combined with an incredible combat sagacity. As a strategist, he had no peer, they said. He possessed the uncanny ability, even if taken by surprise, to assess a situation in an instant and lead his followers in a course of action that took adva..tage of the greatest vulnerability of the enemy, while at the same time exposing his own followers to the least possible risk. Though an excellent marksman with bow or gun and a fearsome wielder of spear, tomahawk and knife, Tecumseh's most favored weapon in such encounters was, oddly enough, a war club that had been given to him by Chiksika. In his grip it became almost a living force, and dozens, scores, perhaps hundreds of enemies had fallen before it in hand-to-hand combat. Though Tecumseh was now only twenty-two, his fame was spreading to all the Indian nations and many were saying that never, in any tribe, had there ever been a warrior his equal.

Now, with Tecumseh approaching at last, it was Spemica Lawba who leaped to the back of his bay gelding and thundered off to be first to welcome him home. Calling Tecumseh's name all the way, he reined to a reckless stop beside his uncle's horse, which was nervously prancing at the exuberant approach. He almost threw himself at Tecumseh in his anxiousness to embrace him. It knocked them both off balance so badly that they toppled from their horses in a heap into the prairie grass, and then scrambled to their feet hugging each other and laughing and thumping each other's backs.

By this time others from the village were riding or running up to them, and there was a long period of enthusiastic greetings. And there were many who, for the first time, noted the striking similarity of appearance between the uncle and his nephew, who was six years younger. But there was also, in spite of all the laughter and gaiety, a vague undercurrent of concern.

Tecumseh and Chiksika had gone away together and now only Tecumseh had returned. Where was Chiksika?

It all came out later.

An impromptu feast was held in celebration of Tecumseh's return and Catahecassa, still principal chief of the tribe, officially welcomed him home, gripping Tecumseh's shoulders with gnarled hands, filled with deep pleasure at the reunion and his eyes soft, his lips curved in a smile as he regarded the young Shawnee and noted the changes that had occurred in him during his absence. Tecumseh's personal appearance was uncommonly fine, for though he was not particularly tall — three inches less than six feet — he had a fitness and symmetry about him that made him stand out at once in any group. His face was oval rather than angular, his nose straight and well formed. His eyes were a clear and nearly transparent hazel, his gaze direct, and his complexion was a smooth and unblemished tan. The hair which fell to just below his broad shoulders was a glossy black, and his arms and legs were straight and well made.

The clothing he wore complemented him in every respect. His basic garments, pullover shirt and leggins, were of the finest, softest doeskin worked to a pleasing sepia tone, the hems and seams accurately cut into frills an inch or so in length. Held in his wide elkhide belt were his primary weapons: an elegant silver-mounted tomahawk, an excellent nine-inch razor-edged knife in a strong leather sheath, and the fine war club Chiksika had given him — a war club fashioned of a heavy smooth stone the size and shape of a large goose egg sewn into wet rawhide which had dried and tightened around it to a hard finish, with a strip of this same rawhide covering a strong hickory handle. Upon his feet he wore very soft but sturdy buffalohide moccasins.

The voice of Catahecassa — Black Hoof — was grave as he addressed this impressive warrior for the first time in three years.

"Moneto has been kind to bring you back safely to your peo-

ple. You went away from us little more than a boy and have
returned a man, with the stories of your exploits in the lands
south of the Can-tuc-kee lands preceding you. It is well. You
have shown the Cherokees that the Shawnee is a great warrior
and your nation is well pleased with you. All of your people
grieve with you over the death of Chiksika, who was also a good
man and fine warrior. His loss is deeply felt. I speak for all of
the Shawnees when I say welcome home, Tecumseh."

For hours after that, Tecumseh related to an enthralled audience the adventures he and Chiksika had experienced since their
departure. They had gone first to the north and west and stayed
for several months with the Miamis, made welcome by the Miami
principal chief, Michikiniqua — Little Turtle. Then they had
moved on and visited the villages of Weas and Muncies, Kickapoos and Piankeshaws, Ottawas and Potawatomies and Winnebagoes. Finally they had stopped and spent nearly a year with
the Sacs and Foxes on the Missitheepi and had gone far west of
that great river with them on their hunts into the lands of endless prairies where the herds of bison were so vast that it took
the great lumbering animals hours to pass a given spot. Eventually they had left the Sacs and Foxes and swung widely to the
south, hunting as they traveled. At one point, just as Chiksika
had several days before predicted would occur, Tecumseh had
been thrown from his horse and suffered a broken hip and they
had camped for many weeks while the injury healed. Later they
visited the Cherokees in the western Tennessee Country, found
them embroiled in a desperate struggle against encroaching
whites, and joined them in their fight. It was then that Tecumseh's phenomenal abilities as warrior came to the fore. There
was a time of great sadness when, on the night before a skirmish
with whites, Chiksika had predicted his own death the next day,
and though Tecumseh had ridden close beside him that day in
an effort to protect him, it was to no avail. A stray rifle ball
from the whites, shot from much too far away to have accurately found its mark, accidentally struck Chiksika in the center

of the forehead and killed him. Tecumseh's grief had been monumental. Afterwards, Tecumseh stayed on with the Cherokees
for almost another year, quickly becoming a leader and strategist
of great ability. And now, at last, he had come home.

Much later that night, long after all the others were asleep,
Spemica Lawba and Tecumseh sat together and spoke of many
things. The nephew told his uncle of his captivity and of his
adoption by Benjamin Logan and of having been given the name
Johnny Logan. He spoke warmly of his eventual joyous reunion
with his mother, Tecumseh's sister, Tecumapese. And he told
him as well of the matters of importance that had occurred in
the Ohio Country since Tecumseh's departure; matters that dealt
mostly with acquisition of Indian lands by the whites.

The British Colonies had now become states and the British
in North America were largely confined to Canada. The fledgling United States government had passed a legislative measure
called the Ordinance of 1787, by which the Northwest Territory had been created, taking in all the Shawnee territory and
much more. It stretched from the Spaylaywitheepi in the south
to the Great Lakes in the north, and from the Missitheepi in the
west to the Pennsylvania boundary in the east. From this vast
expanse of territory, at least three states were eventually to be
formed, to be called Ohio, Indiana and Illinois. Later, if deemed
advisable, these would be broken down further to create two
more states, to be called Michigan and Wisconsin.

A general named Arthur St. Clair had been appointed governor of the Ohio Country and already he was breaking it down
into counties. A military installation called Fort Harmar had been
constructed on the north side of the river in the Ohio Country,
at the mouth of the Muskingum River, and then a second one,
called Fort Washington, had been constructed on the north bank
at a little settlement named Losantiville, but which had recently
been renamed Cincinnati. Because the horizons for settlement
were opened, last year alone over twenty thousand settlers had
come down the Spaylaywitheepi, and once again there had been

an upsurge in the unprovoked killings of Indians seen along the riverbanks and, in retaliation, an upsurge in the raids by Shawnees, Miamis and the warriors of other tribes against the encroachers. The great white chief in the East, President George Washington, chose to largely ignore the insults, harassment and devastation brought down upon the Shawnees by the flood of new settlers, but he became incensed when the Shawnees retaliated and he learned that hundreds of settlers had been killed and their homesteads burned. That was when he had instructed Governor St. Clair to send out an expedition to castigate the Indians. St. Clair had selected an ambitious general named Josiah Harmar to lead that expedition. Harmar was at this very moment assembling and equipping his army. And to intercept and fight that force, the confederation of tribes had just selected as their leaders, Little Turtle of the Miamis and Blue Jacket of the Shawnees.

The firelight reflected an odd expression in Spemica Lawba's eyes as he concluded his narration to Tecumseh. The youth sighed. "Isn't there some way, Tecumseh, that we can live in peace with the whites? Isn't there some way that we can share with them what we have that they want, while they share with us what they have that we need?"

For some time Tecumseh did not respond, and when he finally shook his head and spoke there was a hollow sadness in his words. "I would like to believe such was possible, nephew," he said, "but I think I would only be deceiving myself. I remember a time when I was just a boy and Chiksika had become a man and I asked of him a very similar question. I have never forgotten his response. He said, 'The white race is a monster who is always hungry and what he eats is land.' It is true. The whites can never be content with only a little; they must have all. And they do not share what they have unless it is on their terms and they expect greater reward in return. It is their way."

Spemica Lawba became upset at the words. "I can't believe that! I can't believe that a true peace between us is not possible.

I have lived with them, Tecumseh," he added earnestly. "I *know* them now. I know that they want peace as much as we do." A far-off look came into his eyes as he continued without pause. "I see a time when we can live together in friendship; a time when, through that friendship, *our* people can learn more of this world, when we can see and experience more of it — not just the woods and prairies where we live! — and the wonderful things about it that we do not know or even suspect. There are so many things we can learn from them, so many comforts to be gained, so many beautiful things we can experience that are denied to us now because we are locked in only one small place in a very large world. And there can be an end to the senseless death and destruction! There are . . ."

He broke off, abruptly abashed at his own passionate outburst, and he saw that Tecumseh was smiling; not a smile of condescension or pity, but more one of understanding.

"You are so much like I was, Spemica Lawba," he said. "There are great ideals burning in your heart and mind, and this is good. Without thinking of such things, without having dreams and goals to make our lives better for all, we will simply gradually die away and even the memory of us will become no more than a shadow, as it was with those who lived in this land before us and who built great mounds of earth and villages of stone." He placed his hand on his nephew's arm and squeezed. He had always felt a great affection for Spemica Lawba, but never so much as now. "I would not dissuade you from your ideals, but what you see, I think, is what you *wish* to be and which, sad to say, can probably never come to pass."

He looked for a long quiet moment at the fire, which was now burning low, then added softly: "I, too, have harbored dreams for our people, and perhaps mine are no less wishes than yours, but I think not." Unexpectedly, he leaned to one side and picked up a slender brittle branch and handed it to the youth. "Break this and throw it onto the fire," he said.

Perplexed, Spemica Lawba took the stick, snapped it easily,

and tossed it onto the glowing coals. It browned, blackened, began to smoke, and then abruptly burst into flame, causing dancing shadows to form on the walls of the wegiwa. Tecumseh picked up another dry branch, even thinner, but longer and straighter. This, too, he handed to his nephew.

"Break this in half." Spemica Lawba did so and was about to throw it into the fire when Tecumseh spoke again. "No. Put the two pieces together and break them again."

With little difficulty the youth did as his uncle bade.

"Again."

This time, with four lengths of the wood, it was much more difficult and Spemica Lawba was forced to bend them over his knee to make them break.

"And again."

The boy put the eight shorter pieces together but then shook his head before even trying to break them. "I could not, uncle," he said. "Together they are too strong."

"Yes!" Tecumseh hissed, his eyes alight now. "Together they are too strong. People are like that too. Singly or in small groups they can be broken, but standing together they cannot be. There is a great lesson in that for us. I told you that I, too, have harbored dreams for our people. One such dream is that if they are brought together and remain together without wavering, they will not be broken, despite whatever force an enemy might bring against them. I see, one day, our people brought together like this."

Spemica Lawba nodded slowly. "By a great chief?"

"Perhaps."

"But that would have to be by a great *principal* chief, Tecumseh." His gaze shifted away and settled on the vestiges of the burning stick. He tossed the lengths of wood still in his hands onto the fire and remained silent until they burst into flame. "Forgive me, uncle, for saying it," he said at length, still not looking at the man, "but though you are a great warrior, you are not a great principal chief and you can never become one.

We are of the Kispokotha sept, you and I, and by our tribal traditions only Chalahgawthas and Thawegilas can become principal chiefs of our people."

"That is true, and tradition must not be arbitrarily broken; yet there are times when tradition can bind people more strongly than thongs. It cannot be yet, but perhaps one day, after grave consideration, it will be recognized that this is a tradition that may do us more harm than good. For now, we must concern ourselves with immediate problems. It is late and we should sleep. In days to come I will put myself under Blue Jacket to strike the army this General Harmar is bringing against us. I have no doubt that you will do this also."

He did not wait for an answer, but came to his feet and strode to his pallet in the corner of the wegiwa where he stripped off his clothing and moccasins, stretched out upon the thick fur of a buffalo robe, composed himself, and was almost immediately asleep.

The youth remained sitting by the fire for a while, grateful that he had not been required to answer his uncle's final comment. He did not wish to fight the Shemanese, had promised that he would not, and now the time was all too swiftly coming when he would have to make a decision that might alter his entire life.

Spemica Lawba — Johnny Logan — was deeply troubled.

CHAPTER VI

October 28, 1790

T HE MISFORTUNE that struck Spemica Lawba early this month turned out to be a blessing in disguise. Before October was a week old, the young Shawnee was stricken with a terrible illness. He was not the only one. At least three dozen other men, women and children were similarly afflicted. For the first three days he felt terrible, vomited frequently, and had a slight fever. It was only the beginning. On the fourth day of the illness the fever heightened drastically and he lay groaning, tended constantly by Tecumapese, who bathed him frequently with cool water brought from the creek and who tried to restrain him and keep him from hurting himself as he thrashed about in intermittent delirium. He could eat nothing, and though a raging thirst besieged him, most of the water given him to drink refused to stay in his stomach.

For four full days the fever raged in him, and finally a crisis point was reached. It seemed certain he would die, as half a dozen others in the village already had, but then the fever broke, the crisis was past, and he fell into a deep sleep. It was still two days more before he could begin to take solid food again and he looked terrible, having lost a great deal of weight and his eyes sunken and discolored from his ordeal. His color came back quickly, his strength much less swiftly. It was fully another five days before he was able to get back to his feet and move about, still very weak but improving steadily. By then it was much too late for him to join — or refuse to join — the expedition; too late for him to have to make that painful decision that so troubled him.

Earlier in the month, on the seventh day, General Josiah Harmar led his army of well over fourteen hundred soldiers — three hundred twenty regulars of the United States Army and eleven hundred thirty-three militia, mainly from Kentucky — out of Fort Washington at Cincinnati and headed northward to engage the Indians.

On the tenth, at about the time Spemica Lawba had just entered the worst phase of his illness, Shawnee spies brought word to Blue Jacket and Little Turtle that the army was coming, and immediately the call was sent out by runners to the various villages for the warriors to take up their arms and rendezvous with the Miami warriors at the place where the St. Joseph River and St. Marys River converged to form the Maumee River. A trading post was there, part of a small settlement called Miamitown. The post was owned by a young British trader named John Kinzie — the man who, three and a half years before, had rescued two bedraggled young women who had escaped Indian captivity and had taken them to Detroit with him. These two young women had been known as Kisahthoi and Tebethto but were actually Margaret and Elizabeth McKenzie; one of whom, Margaret, he soon married, while the other married his partner, John Clark. The Miamitown settlement, close to the principal village of the Miamis, Kekionga, was chosen as the rendezvous point because it was believed that Kinzie would provide them with arms and ammunition and other supplies for the forthcoming conflict.

By the twelfth of the month, Harmar's own spies brought word of the Indian rendezvous occurring at Miamitown and this immediately became the expedition's target.

Spemica Lawba, willing or not, of course could not answer

the call for warriors, nor could a great many similarly ill warriors from his own and other villages. And there were many warriors not themselves stricken who could not answer the summons because their wives and children had the illness and required constant tending. The Miamis, Potawatomies and other tribes were also smitten by the sickness and, as a result, the number of Indians who ultimately rendezvoused at Miamitown was disappointingly small — just over one hundred twenty warriors. How could so few possibly oppose a much better armed army of over fourteen hundred fifty soldiers? Even when a detachment of some thirty Sacs and Foxes showed up at the rendezvous, the odds remained a staggering nine to one against the Indians.

In Wapatomica and other Shawnee villages, those who were left behind — Spemica Lawba among them — waited fearfully for news. Today that wait ended. Still feeling a little drained but nearly back to normal again, Spemica Lawba was overjoyed suddenly to see the party of horsemen approaching Wapatomica with the victory cry erupting from their throats. Forty-eight warriors from Wapatomica had ridden away for the rendezvous and now forty-eight were returning, with Wasegoboah, Tecumseh, Sauwaseekau, Kumskaka and Lowawluwaysica among them.

There were wonderul reunions, and then everyone crowded into the great room of the *msi-kah-mi-qui* to hear what had happened, and the jubilation that swept through them was like nothing they had even before experienced. The victory over the powerful force of General Harmar was complete and the prevailing feeling was that now perhaps the Americans had been taught a lesson that would make them reconsider well before ever again invading the Indian territory with an army.

Warrior after warrior rose to speak, the audience clinging in fascination to every word. Bit by bit the events that had occurred became clear. The small force of Indians under Blue Jacket and Little Turtle, realizing the ridiculousness of attempting to engage the large army head-on, had watched and waited, biding their time for the best possible opportunity. They had watched as the American force approached Miamitown, watched as it entered and destroyed not only Kekionga but several other abandoned villages as well, watched as they destroyed some fifteen thousand bushels of corn the Indians had worked so hard to harvest, along with much of the vegetable crop. Seething inside, they watched as the army looted and then burned John Kinzie's trading post. They watched and waited . . . waiting for Josiah Harmar to make a mistake, and eventually they were rewarded.

Harmar had stupidly and unnecessarily split his force and sent out a detachment. The Indians struck it hard, killing twenty-two men and putting the remainder to flight. When the American survivors reached the main army and reported, it was expected that Harmar would immediately launch a powerful counterattack. Instead, he retreated. At last, bowing to the angry demands of his own men, he consented to allow another detachment — under Colonel John Hardin — to leave the army in order to return to the site of the attack to bury the dead. It was a second mistake quickly parlayed into another victory even better than the first.

Michikiniqua and Blue Jacket swept down upon them in so ferocious an assault that the detachment under Hardin could not recover. What little resistance they formed was quickly beaten down, and the survivors fled back to the main army with the tragic news. Again the army expected General Harmar would turn back and lead a massive relatiatory assault, but the commander's backbone had turned to jelly and he ordered an immediate retreat to Fort Washington, leaving in such haste that many crucial supplies were abandoned.

The combined statistics for the two battles were, for the Indians, seven men wounded, three killed.

The American army left behind a total of one hundred eighty-three men dead.

Jubilantly the Indians had gathered up and divided among

themselves the supplies, weapons, clothing and ammunition left behind by the retreating army, along with a large number of packhorses.

So far as was known, only one captive was taken by the army — a little eleven-year-old Maykujay Shawnee girl whose only living relative, her father, had been one of the Indian fatalities. She had been found cowering in the corner of one of the wegiwas the army had destroyed before the battles. The Indians who had been watching from hiding saw her taken away, but there was nothing they could do about it.

Her name was Pskipahcah Ouiskelotha — The Bluebird.

Spemica Lawba remembered having seen her once or twice during visits to her little village, but he did not really know her. Nevertheless, he silently wished her well, hoping that her treatment in the hands of the Shemanese would be as gentle and uplifting as his had been.

The returned warriors continued to relate other facets of the conflict, and the euphoria that settled over the warriors was all-encompassing. The taste of victory was in the mouths of the Shawnees, and it was a taste to be savored.

CHAPTER VII

October 30, 1790

HE LITTLE Shawnee Indian girl was infinitely weary and, even worse, desperately afraid, yet only a little of how she felt was evident in her attitude. She found some security in clinging to the officer and had taken to burying her face in his chest whenever one of the other riders came near. He was the enemy, true, but in the days that had passed since her captivity, he had treated her kindly, fed her, cared for her, protected her from any harm from the other soldiers throughout the dreadful ride south. Now the defeated army was approaching a huge settlement.

The colonel reined up for a moment to rest his horse atop a hill overlooking a huge river. A multitude of buildings were below them, many of them log cabins, but quite a few sturdily constructed of red brick and fronting on wide, neatly laid-out streets which were a bustle of activity, with carriages and people on foot moving to and fro. A large fort enclosed by high pickets sharpened to points at their tops dominated the scene, its gates guarded by men in uniform. At the foot of the town, on the north bank of the river the girl had never seen before but which she knew to be the Spaylaywitheepi, a number of boats and rafts tied to broad docks were being unloaded. A pall of wood smoke overhung the whole scene, and the officer pointed at the young city.

"Cincinnati," he said.

Pskipahcah Ouiskelotha did not know the word, but this place was evidently their destination and her fear increased sharply. Among the Shawnee towns the arrival of a new captive almost always meant that the residents — men, women and children — turned out and, armed with a variety of sturdy sticks and limber switches, quickly formed a double line through which the newly arrived prisoner would have to run, trying to avoid the blows raining down upon him as he ran. Normally such a gauntlet line ended at the *msi-kah-mi-qui*, and if the prisoner could reach that structure he would be safe, but frequently the blows became too much and the prisoner faltered, fell, and was beaten to death before he could reach the structure.

Below, there was no indication of a gauntlet line being formed, but that did little to assuage Pskipahcah Ouiskelotha's fears. She envisioned being tied to a post and burned or run through by a sword or having her head chopped off. She thought it was only a matter of time and she tried to be brave, but the fear remained strong in her and she trembled. The man felt it and he gripped her gently and held her a little away from him so he could see her face.

"I don't know your name, yet, little girl," Colonel John Hardin said softly, "but I'll soon find out. I know you can't understand me, but maybe you can get the feel of what I'm saying. You're afraid, but you don't have to be. No one will hurt you. You are one of the prettiest little girls I have ever seen anywhere. I am taking you to my home where you will meet my wife and my children, and they will welcome you and love you. You will live with us, become our daughter, and our family will be your family. No one will ever harm you."

Abruptly she buried her face against his chest again and he chuckled and put his horse into motion. She had no idea what the words meant that he had spoken to her, but they sounded as friendly as he had looked and been since he had taken her from the soldiers who had discovered her hiding in the wegiwa. Was this, she wondered, how the Shemanese treated their prisoners before killing them?

Pskipahcah Ouiskelotha was still very much afraid.

CHAPTER VIII

November 1, 1790

PEMICA LAWBA, still showing some of the gauntness his illness had engendered, sat beside his uncle in the wegiwa and felt a wash of sympathy rise in him as Tecumseh pulled the blanket closer around his shoulders to ward off the chill. The season's first significant cold snap had arrived, and Tecumseh's long sojourn in the south had evidently made him unaccustomed to the raw wind and bone-penetrating chill, of northern Ohio.

Only two other people were in the wegiwa with them, and Spemica Lawba felt a little awed at being in their presence. One of them was Catahecassa — Black Hoof — principal chief of the Shawnees, in whose wegiwa this private council was being held. The other was Weh-yeh-pih-ehr-sehn-wah — Blue Jacket — war chief of the Shawnees and successor of Moluntha as principal chief of the Maykujay sept. Since Spemica Lawba lived in the same village as Black Hoof, he was reasonably familiar with seeing the chief, but he had seen Blue Jacket only from a distance on rare occasions and had never before conversed with him. He was in awe of the famed warrior, the more so since Blue Jacket had shared leadership with Little Turtle of the small Indian force that had so wisely and effectively decimated the army of General Josiah Harmar, knowing in his own heart that he could never become a warrior like that, especially against the Shemanese.

The very fact that Spemica Lawba had been honored with the privilege of sitting in on this meeting was wholly attributable to Tecumseh, who had insisted upon it, saying, "I know of no other Shawnee his age or even considerably older who is so sensitive to both the problems of his own people and those of the Shemanese, nor one who ponders to such extent in an effort to resolve the differences between us. He has not yet been disillusioned at the hopelessness of any sort of equitable coexistence occurring between us. And who is to say he is incorrect? Perhaps he envisions things which others of us cannot. However this may be, he is wise beyond his years and his presence in our council could only be of benefit." Thus it was that Spemica Lawba had been invited to attend and was on hand now, seated beside his uncle.

Tecumseh relighted his pipe, listening closely as Blue Jacket continued recounting the details of the fight. He was evidently impressed with the sharpness of detail and accuracy of the war chief's account. Blue Jacket neither boasted nor exaggerated regarding any aspect of the encounter and it was obvious that he was far more deeply affected with sorrow at the few warrior deaths that had occurred in the two battles than at the relatively great number of enemies who had been slain. Nevertheless, it had been a most significant victory and, when he was finished, Catahecassa was lavish in praise of the Maykujay chief's leadership. Tecumseh also praised him.

Blue Jacket smiled, acknowledging the compliments with pleasure. He, too, lighted a pipe and then he faced Spemica Lawba's uncle, his countenance serious. "I have my own thoughts about it, and we have heard Catahecassa's views, but I would like to have yours as well, Tecumseh. The words of one whose fame as a warrior has spread so far among so many tribes could be of great value. Do you think the Shemanese have now been taught a lesson and will cease their attempts to take our lands?" Peripherally, Tecumseh saw that his nephew was looking at him intently, but he kept his eyes on Blue Jacket. "I think, Weh-yeh-pih-ehr-sehn-wah," he said slowly, "that we have scarcely begun to see the intensity of the Americans' desire for our lands, just as we have scarcely begun to see the strength of arms they are capable of bringing against us. No barrier will stop them. For many years our people thought the mountains to the east would check their expansion, but they did not. Then it was believed, after they came into the Can-tuc-kee lands, that the Spaylaywitheepi would be a barrier they would never cross, but they have crossed it and they have built their forts and towns at the southern edge of the Ohio Country and for them this is only a beginning. Our tribe split some years ago, with the majority migrating westward of the Missitheepi, confident that the great grandmother of rivers would be a barrier beyond which they would not penetrate. But I know in my heart they will eventually step across it as if it were nothing more than a small stream." He nodded slowly, sadly, and concluded with bitterness. "Yes, I think the Shemanese will return; they will come against us with a larger and much stronger army than before, and perhaps with a better leader."

"I hope they don't," Spemica Lawba blurted, then dropped his eyes for having had the temerity to speak without being recognized.

"We all hope they don't," Blue Jacket responded dryly, "but our reasons may differ from yours. Would it be because you lived with them for some time that you now wish they would not attack again?"

The youth raised his head and looked at the chief directly, a faintly smoldering defiance in his eyes. "I do not hate them," he said. "I wish they would stay where they are and we where we are and that there could be peace between us. They are not all bad people."

"No people," Tecumseh put in, faintly amused, "are all bad; just as none are all good."

"I agree." It was Catahecassa who spoke, and instantly they deferred to him giving him all their attention. "With Tecumseh as well as with Spemica Lawba," he added, "it is too easy to judge an enemy as all bad, when it may be only his leaders who are so. It is also easy," he looked pointedly at Spemica Lawba, "to be taken in by the good will of a few and mistake this for the feelings of all. In all respects, we owe it to ourselves and to those who will come after us to view with the greatest possibly clarity the motives and ultimate goals of all those with whom we deal, whether friends or enemies." His gaze shifted to Tecumseh, then to Blue Jacket. "You are a great war chief, Weh-yeh-pih-ehr-sehn-wah, and you are passionate, as well you should be, about defending ourselves with the tomahawk. Because it happened so many years ago, there are those among the Shawnee who have forgotten that you were born to the Shemanese; that you were raised by them to young manhood and that you were captured as a youth not much older than he," he indicated Spemica Lawba, "and were adopted into our tribe. None of us then had any idea that you would one day become one of our greatest chiefs. The ways of the whites, therefore, are familiar to you and if any one of us should be able to divine what the whites mean to do, it should be you. And you, as all of us know, are strong in your denunciation of them and in your determination to meet them with tomahawk and war club at every turn.

"We all," he continued, "tend to think of the Shemanese as our greatest foe, whose sole desire is to uproot us from our lands and to destroy us if we attempt to thwart them. This we cannot allow to happen and, if necessary, we must fight them to prevent it. At one and the same time," his eyes moved back to Spemica Lawba, "we must not overlook the wisdom that might be brought to us by one who has also lived among them, but more recently, and learned more than we of their present ways

and inclinations. If there is any possibility of a true peace between us, a sharing of our cultures on an equal basis for the
benefit of both, then this should be a goal to strive for with all
our will."

The principal chief fell silent for a moment, but no one spoke,
knowing he was not yet finished. The heavily built chief sucked
on his pipestem, but the pipe had gone out, and he leaned forward and thrust the end of a small branch into the fire and relighted the tobacco with the flame that appeared on the end of
the stick. After he had puffed several times and wisps of smoke
formed drifting tendrils, he frowned faintly and spoke again.

"I yearn for peace for our people. I have long believed that a
desired and acceptable future for the Shawnees must be brought
about more through following the path of peace than the path
of war. Yet, we must not delude outselves. We are all aware
that many peace treaties have been made in the past and none —
not one! — has been honored for long by the whites. If we can
be assured that allying ourselves to these Shemanese, these
Americans, is in our best interest for our future, then all possible
effort must be made in this direction. But," he added, his eyes
narrowing, "if it cannot be and their leaders choose the rocky
path of war, they will find we will not stand aside."

Catahecassa was obviously finished speaking, and Spemica
Lawba, steeling himself for the possibility of disapproval, was
first to speak. "If General Logan is one of those leaders," he
stated firmly, "he would not choose to make war against us. He
is a good man!"

"From what you have told us," Tecumseh responded, "the
General Logan who took you *was* a good man. But, in your
admiration, do not be blinded to the fact that he led the army
who came and destroyed Mackachack and twelve others of our
towns. I do not know if he, personally, wishes to have our lands,
but the Shemanese mostly do and we must oppose this."

Spemica Lawba nodded miserably. "I understand that, but I

do not wish to fight against General Logan. I have told him I would never do so."

"It was a promise you should not have made," Blue Jacket put in, an edge to his words.

"But one," Tecumseh said, speaking to the war chief, "that a person of honor would have made; that you would have made, Weh-yeh-pih-ehr-sehn-wah, or I, under similar circumstances." He turned to gaze at his nephew. "I hope the time may never come when you will encounter him in war."

And Spemica Lawba, with all his heart, hoped the same.

CHAPTER IX

November 2, 1791

I T WAS THE first time Spemica Lawba had worn white man's garb since his return to the Shawnees and he felt strange in the clothing. It was much less comfortable than he remembered, partly because of being somewhat too small for him. Until some two weeks ago, these were the same clothes that Tecumseh had worn on a number of occasions and they had seemed to fit him quite well. Spemica Lawba, however, had grown inches in the past year and had filled out considerably, to the extent that now, on the threshold of entering his eighteenth year, he appeared to be far more a man than a boy. He felt awkward and obvious, though actually he was neither. The feeling was engendered more by what he was doing than what he was wearing, since he was presently engaged in a very dangerous pursuit.

He was a spy.

When Wasegoboah and Tecumseh left here to pace St. Clair's army and spy on it, they had left Spemica Lawba behind with a specific and important mission: he was to determine when the anticipated army reinforcements would arrive or, if they showed up, to carry the news to Blue Jacket and Little Turtle immediately. A great deal might hinge on receiving that vital information.

For weeks the three, along with half a dozen other Shawnees, had spied on Cincinnati generally and Fort Washington specifically. An expedition against the confederated tribes, especially the Shawnees and Miamis, had been ordered by the President to commence in August to chastise the Indians and regain some of the prestige lost with Harmar's inglorious defeat and retreat. Soon after that disastrous campaign, Harmar had resigned his commission, thereby saving the government the necessity of discharging him. Governor-General Arthur St. Clair had been named to head this newest campaign. All spring and summer St. Clair had built up his force at Fort Washington, eager to be on the march, but promised reinforcements and supplies had not arrived from Pittsburgh and the departure had been delayed. Week after week passed while the frustrated commander and his army waited. Very soon a point was reached where, if St. Clair did not go ahead and march with the men and equipment he had on hand, the winter would close in and the campaign would have to be postponed until the following year. And so, finally, St. Clair had led his men out of Cincinnati on September 17 and headed north, leaving behind a skeleton garrison at Fort Washington with orders to forward the reinforcement troops and supplies as soon as they arrived.

It was during the final weeks that the Shawnee spying party, led by Tecumseh, took up their surveillance. He had stationed Wasegoboah and Spemica Lawba to watch the perimeter of the town and had himself dressed in purloined clothing of the whites and entered the town. Each evening the little party of Indian spies would rendezvous at a secret camp a few miles from Cincinnati to discuss what had been discovered, and at intervals Tecumseh would send one of the Shawnees as runner to the Indian forces to divulge whatever intelligence had been gathered. That main encampment of the combined Indian forces — upwards of three thousand warriors — was camped well over one hundred miles north of them, at a point where the Auglaize River emptied into the Maumee. So successful had Tecumseh been in his disguise that he had even entered Fort Washington on a few occasions without detection. When the army finally moved out fifteen days ago, Tecumseh had sent one of his last remaining spies with news of it to the main encampment of the Indians. Then, discarding the disguise, he and the others who were left set out to pace and observe the army from hiding, leaving Spemica Lawba behind with his solitary spying mission. The young man's uncle and stepfather had no idea, however, that Spemica Lawba would gather up the clothing discarded by Tecumseh and enter the town as Tecumseh had.

Now, as Johnny Logan, he walked about the docks at Cincinnati as if he belonged there, moving purposefully from one point to another, listening to bits and snatches of conversation and reading notices posted on trees or on the sides of sheds. He was relatively inconspicuous, as the wharves seemed to be a popular place for loitering or for finding temporary employment. Earlier today he had moved about the same way for several hours in the main part of town closer to Fort Washington. The initial intense nervousness he had experienced in his role of intrigue had more or less faded, but he was still not wholly at ease.

In mid-afternoon a fairly large, well-built boat hove into view up the Spaylaywitheepi. He watched closely, and in just over half an hour the boat slid smoothly into moorage at the broadly planked wharf where he was standing. Large though it was, he decided it could hardly be the craft carrying the expected army reinforcements that were so long overdue. He almost changed his mind about that when the first person to disembark was a United States Army officer of very snappy appearance. The officer strode toward the town with brisk pace, giving Johnny Logan a brief glance and curt nod as he passed, evidently in no manner suspicious that the young man was anything more than he appeared to be — just another of the hangers-on at the docks.

A number of other passengers had also disembarked, and after they had passed him en route to town, Johnny sauntered over to the boat. Its captain was a bearded man of about sixty with rheumy eyes, heavily veined nose and blotchy skin. He was directing the efforts of a pair of workers who were carrying baggage and a variety of goods from the deck to the wharf.

"Need another hand to help with the unloading?" Johnny asked.

"Can't afford another, but even if I could," the captain jerked his head toward the pair of deckhands, "there ain't nothin' aboard that these two can't handle. Anything excitin' been going on around here?"

The young man shrugged. "A few things, I guess."

"Such as what?" As with most of the boatmen, the captain was a gatherer and dispenser of news and he was eager to talk.

"Well, St. Clair finally headed north with his army." He licked his lips and decided to try some subtlety in an effort to get some information out of the man. "He got tired of waiting for —"

"How many soldiers did he have?"

"Fourteen hundred."

"All militia?"

Johnny Logan recalled the figures that Tecumseh had told them at their secret camp. "Uh . . . no. About half and half, regulars and militia."

The captain chuckled. "Wait'll that soldier-boy I brung downriver hears that. He ain't gonna be happy a-tall. He was all fired up for goin' along on St. Clair's campaign."

"Who was he?" Johnny asked, thinking the information might prove of value.

"Said his name was Harrison. Newly appointed to his rank by the President hisself, he said. 'I am Ensign William Henry Harrison, sir,' as he put it. Stiff sort of young feller. Sure liked to put on airs. Took hisself very serious, he did."

The name meant nothing to Johnny Logan and so he went back to what he had been saying. "Anyway, St. Clair got tired of waiting for those reinforcements that were supposed to come. 'Spect they'll be showing up in another day or —"

"Howdy." This second interruption came from another of the

loiterers who had walked up to them, an unkempt individual with a perceptible limp. "You doing any hirin'?" When the captain shook his head and gave him essentially the same reply he had given Johnny, the untidy man shrugged, not caring one way or another. "Where you out of?" he asked the captain.

"Pittsburgh. Stopped off at Fort Randolph an' Fort Harmar."

"See any Injens along the way?"

"Nope. Don't much see 'em anymores. Usta' was you c'd git a shot off at 'em at ever' other bend or so. Not no more."

Johnny Logan felt his stomach churning but he managed to keep his face expressionless.

The loiterer sniffed. "Mebbe you ain't done shootin' at 'em yet."

The boatman looked at him sharply. "Now what's that s'posed to mean?"

"It means St. Clair's likely to get his fanny whupped. I reckon," he said, glancing at Johnny. "You already heard 'bout it, but he ain't." He looked back at the bearded man. "They was 'bout three hunnerd of St. Clair's militia deserted a few nights after they left here. St. Clair didn't find out till the next mornin'. So right away he sent off a hunnered an' forty of his regulars under Major Hamtramck to chase 'em and bring 'em back. Hamtramck followed 'em to the river an' over into Kaintuck and he ain't come back yet. Way I figger it, St. Clair, he ain't gonna have much more'n a thousan' men to hit them Injens with an' the spies say the Injens got mebbe two-three thousan' war-painted bucks rarin' t'go." He shook his head. "I'll tell you, I was with Harmar when he had t' tuck his tail 'twixt his legs an' run all the way back here — that's where I got this bad leg — an' I'm sure glad I ain't with St. Clair now."

Johnny saw his opportunity and leaped upon it. "Might not be as bad as you think," he said. "The reinforcements'll be here in a day or two with the supplies an' they'll catch up to St. Clair."

"Ain't so!" interjected the bearded boatman. He spat a brown stream down into the muddy water of the river. "Ain't no way them reinforcements an' supplies'll ever get here in time t' help him. Hell, they was only beginnin' t' git organized in Pittsburgh the day I left there. Said they didn't figger they'd be able to leave there for at least three-four weeks!"

The conversation continued, and Johnny Logan waited a short while before telling them he had to leave. They hardly paid any attention to his departure. Nevertheless, it was only with great effort that he restrained himself from breaking into a run as he headed for the secluded camp where he had a pair of horses waiting to carry him without delay to the main Indian encampment.

Spemica Lawba's first spying mission had turned out to be a great success.

CHAPTER X

November 7, 1791

A S SPEMICA LAWBA reached Wapatomica, he found the Shawnee town in the midst of the most extravagant celebration he had ever witnessed among his people. A great roaring fire sent plumes of billowing smoke high into the crisp November blue sky. Several hundred warriors — many of them with the war paint still on their faces — and half again that many women and children pranced and leaped and danced around the fire, and here and there warriors reenacted their roles in the battle they had fought.

It had been the greatest battle between Indians and whites that the North American continent had ever seen. It had also been the worst defeat the whites had ever suffered in any such battle. Blue Jacket and Little Turtle were being revered as the greatest war chiefs who had ever lived, and all the Indians were in a state of excitement and exultation that bordered on ecstasy.

They welcomed Spemica Lawba with loud cries of greeting and praise for the dangerous spying efforts he had made at Cincinnati, which had been reported to them by Tecumseh and Wasegoboah, both of whom were participating in the celebration. The fact that the final information he had gathered was now of no real consequence made little difference; it was the courage and shrewdness and skill with which he had carried out his mission that was important, and when, as was expected of him, he related the details of how he had donned the white man's clothes that Tecumseh had discarded and entered the town, searching out information, they cheered and hooted with pleasure and admiration.

Little by little, as he listened to the exploits being related and talked privately to his stepfather and uncles, Spemica Lawba was able to piece together the details of what had occurred. St. Clair's army, after leaving Cincinnati — with Tecumseh's party following and spying upon them — had erected a fort on the Great Miami River twenty-three miles north and named it Fort Hamilton. Here St. Clair left a garrison of twenty men and moved on northward another forty-four miles where a second installation — Fort Jefferson — was built and it, too, was garrisoned with twenty men.

By that time the morale of the army, especially the militia, was very low. Upwards of five hundred wives and campfollowers were tagging along, and the militia demanded that they be provided with stores of food. Since the army's supplies had never come and the army was itself on half-rations, St. Clair was justified in refusing to accede to the demand. That was when, after darkness had fallen, some three hundred of the militia deserted, gathering up a sizable segment of their women and heading back for Kentucky. In the morning, a furious St. Clair sent Major Hamtramck at the head of one hundred forty regulars in pursuit.

Weakened by the desertions, by sending out the detachment and by having to leave men to garrison two forts, St. Clair pushed on with only nine hundred twenty men and that was when Tecumseh himself sped on to the main Indian encampment with the news and urged immediate attack at the point where the army would be crossing the upper reaches of the Wabash River.

It had snowed fairly heavily the first two days of November and the attack, brilliantly planned and executed by Blue Jacket and Little Turtle, occurred at dawn on November 4. Hampered by lack of men and supplies, to say nothing of defective rifles and cannon powder that would not ignite, St. Clair's army suffered a shattering defeat. The snow-covered ground had become a macabre scene of blood and bodies. Of the nine hundred twenty Americans involved, only twenty-four men escaped uninjured. Two hundred sixty-four were wounded, and a staggering total of six hundred thirty-two were killed, along with an additional two hundred campfollowers who had still been tagging along.

A total of sixty-six Indians were killed, of which only nineteen were Shawnees.

For the first time an American frontier battle had taken on the proportions of a national disaster, and the victorious Indians had triumphed beyond anything before in their history. Little wonder that a vast jubilation swept the Indian tribes and that here in Wapatomica and in other villages throughout the Northwest Territory stirring victory celebrations were being held that would last for days.

And in the midst of it all, Spemica Lawba was torn by warring emotions: great happiness for the success of his own people, great sadness for the tragedy that had befallen his adopted people, and frustration that this would undoubtedly be a terrible setback for any hope of the peace he yearned for between the races. There was, however, one element of the affair for which he was extremely grateful: once again Spemica Lawba had been spared the painful decision of what he would do if required to fight the Shemanese.

CHAPTER XI

September 30, 1792

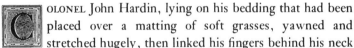 OLONEL John Hardin, lying on his bedding that had been placed over a matting of soft grasses, yawned and stretched hugely, then linked his fingers behind his neck and lay back, staring at the clear starry sky. He was very pleased with himself. Tomorrow he would be in Wapatomica, the capital of the Shawnee nation, conferring with the principal chief of that tribe, Black Hoof — Catahecassa. He felt strongly that he would be able to accomplish what all the previous American emissaries before him had failed to do; that he would accomplish in a quiet way what neither the army of General Harmar nor that of General St. Clair had been able to accomplish by force of arms. He smiled as he thought that one day he might be remembered in history as the man who had brought lasting peace between Indians and whites.

His two Shawnee guides, lying on the opposite side of the campfire, were breathing heavily and obviously asleep. Hardin was grateful for the good fortune that had allowed him accidentally to encounter them early this morning. One had an Indian name he could not pronounce, but which translated into Little Blue Jacket, and who told Hardin in broken English that he was the son of the famed Shawnee war chief. The other man, who perpetually wore a sour expression had a name that meant something like Whirling Dust, which Hardin suspected would translate accurately to Tornado. The two had volunteered to guide him to Wapatomica tomorrow and both had been very helpful in tending to his comfort in camp this evening.

As he looked at the night sky heavily sprinkled with stars, a meteor flashed briefly in a searing white line and he smiled wistfully, wondering if his wife back in Kentucky might be looking at the heavens tonight, too, and might perhaps have seen the same shooting star. Thought of his wife and home also made him think of his son, Thomas, and his adopted daughter, Bluebird.

"Pskipahcah Ouiskelotha."

He whispered her Shawnee name aloud, pleased that he could pronounce it properly, saying it again slowly, and enjoying the way the syllables rolled off his tongue: "Puh-skip-uh-kah . . . Whis-kee-low-tha." What a nice name it was and what a darling girl she had turned out to be. She had been with them now for only a month short of two years and had adapted perfectly to life with the Hardin family, learning to speak English far more rapidly than he had been able to learn a few words of her tongue. He shrugged off his failing and smiled again as he thought of how well she and Tom got along together. He visualized how she was just beginning to develop into a young woman and toyed for a moment with the idea that, as time passed, she and Tom might fall in love and marry. Almost immediately he rejected the thought, not because of any objection to it — it would, in fact, please him — but because he knew Tom was enamored of Ben Logan's daughter and would probably wind up marrying her. Besides, the relationship between Tom and Bluebird had become more of a close brother-and-sister familiarity than anything else. But Bluebird was such a sweet girl and she had brought such beauty and laughter into their lives!

Hardin's thoughts turned to his present mission and he fervently hoped he would succeed. President Washington had personally commissioned him to carry a peace proposal to the

Shawnees, just as William Wells had been commissioned to carry a similar proposal to the Miamis. Wells, whose family had been among the earliest of the Kentucky settlers, had been captured as a boy by the Miamis and adopted into the family of Chief Little Turtle. Recently he had begun resuming his ties with the whites, and the Americans had been relying on him more and more heavily as interpreter and go-between for peace negotiations. But at the same time, the United States government was readying another army to come against the Indians if they refused to agree to peace on the terms suggested by the government. That army, if the time came for it to march, would be commanded by a general far shrewder and far more to be feared by the Indians than Harmar or St. Clair. His name was Anthony Wayne.

Hardin gave a little grunt as he turned on his side, hoping the strife between Indians and Americans could be put to rest diplomatically rather than through warfare. He fell asleep very quickly then, a small smile still on his lips from thinking what a coup it would be if he were able to return with news of the Shawnees having agreed to a solid peace.

John Hardin would have been very surprised had he known that the surly Shawnee he knew as Tornado had recognized him immediately at their meeting as the officer who had carried off Pskipahcah Ouiskelotha, daughter of his brother whom the Shemanese had killed. But Hardin never knew that. During the night, one of the warriors rose silently and buried his tomahawk to the hilt in the officer's head.

CHAPTER XII

December 31, 1794

PEMICA LAWBA, now twenty, was very upset at what was occurring. For several moons a heated battle of words had been going on between Catahecassa and Tecumseh. Now, on this final day of one of the most devastating years in Shawnee history, it appeared that the long vocal battle was coming to an end and there would be no resolution to the problem — only a conclusion that was distressing to all.

The *msi-kah-mi-qui* in Wapatomica was filled with warriors from all the Shawnee villages. They had been listening intently to all that was being said and it was apparent that there was as much a rift between many of them as the one that was ever widening between Tecumseh and the principal chief of the Shawnees.

There was an uncertainty these days in Catahecassa that had never been there before. The events of the past summer had shocked and stunned him and seemed to have taken something vital from him. He still retained the highest position in his tribe, but there seemed to have developed a slight erosion in his powers. Though others may not have noticed it, Spemica Lawba detected an inclination in the chief to be unsure of himself and, in that very uncertainty, to become jealous of his position and fearful that his authority would be usurped.

Now he stood before the assembled warriors and glared at Tecumseh, who sat to one side with Wasegoboah, Spemica Lawba and the two survivors of the triplets, Kumskaka and Lowawluwaysica.

"You, Tecumseh," he said angrily, "have no right to cause dissension in the tribe. You have no right to make our warriors question the wisdom of what I feel to be right for our people. And in view of what has so recently occurred at Fallen Timbers, you have no basis for not acquiescing in a course that will bring us lasting peace. You may reply to what I have said."

Tecumseh came to his feet, facing the chief who remained standing in place. "What I have said, Catahecassa," he responded firmly, his strong voice carrying well to all in attendance, "has not been said for the purpose of causing dissension. Nevertheless, if I believe in my heart that the course we are following is wrong and will damage us, then I have every right, as well as an obligation, to express my feelings and suggest what I believe to be more appropriate alternatives. I have never been in favor of not having peace — in fact, I have advocated it — but to agree to *any* peace that robs us of the lands where our fathers are buried, that strips from us our dignity, our pride and self-esteem and forces us to live without honor, is something I cannot do. That there are others among us who feel the same is no surprise to me. What they do must be what their *own* hearts tell them to do. I do not attempt to coerce them one way or the other; I tell them only how I feel and what course I will take. And what I have told them is this: I cannot agree to sign such a peace."

"We have no choice, Tecumseh," Catahecassa said.

Tecumseh shook his head. "So long as we are alive, we have a choice."

It was an impasse for the moment, and to preserve his dignity, Catahecassa chose not to reply. Instead, he faced the large audience and raised his arms. "It is time," he said, "for thought. We will smoke."

Immediately there was a shuffling and murmur as men began filling their pipes with *kinnikinnick*, the Indian tobacco made of a mixture of properly cured herbs, including willow leaves. Spemica Lawba did so also, not joining in the murmur of conversation but withdrawing into himself, disturbed by the dangerous rift and the disastrous year that had caused it.

The defeat of St. Clair, though a tremendous victory for the Indians and a decided setback to the Americans, in no way diverted the latter from their desire for Indian lands. It only made them more cautious and more determined to avoid the mistakes of the past. Kentucky had become a state in 1792 and now boasted a huge population of whites, with more coming all the time. Emissaries of peace sent among the tribes by the President were universally unsuccessful. In exchange for guarantees of peace, the United States demanded vast concessions of land, suggesting that the Indians who occupied them move west of the Mississippi. That on the one hand this meant leaving their homelands and hunting grounds and, on the other, moving into strange areas populated with tribes that were traditional enemies, was of little concern to the government. In fact General Wayne was slowly but very methodically building up a strong, highly disciplined and well-trained army to move against them as soon as he felt himself ready to do so.

The British in Canada, as they had been doing ever since the Revolution, continued making overtures of peace and extending promises of aid to the Indians in their struggle against the Americans. Detroit was still in British hands, though now legally a part of the United States, and the British there quietly moved into the Maumee Valley of Ohio and built a fortification called Fort Miami, garrisoned with British soldiers. Should there come another outbreak of war between the Indians and Americans, the British implied, arms and ammunition, food and clothing and protection would be given to the Indians by the British. They were also strong in their hints that British soldiers would fight beside the Indians against the Americans.

Skirmishes still continued to occur throughout the Ohio, Indiana and Illinois territories, but General Wayne refused to be provoked into a fight until he was ready. With his new aide-de-camp, William Henry Harrison, always on hand, Wayne ordered the construction of a very strong new fort not many miles from where St. Clair had been so devastatingly defeated. He named it Fort Greenville. A detachment was sent out to gather up and bury the bones of those who died at the St. Clair defeat, and when this was accomplished, a fort was built at the site and called Fort Recovery. This put the Americans uncomfortably close to the Shawnee villages and, as a result, many of these villages were abandoned and reestablished farther north in Ohio along the Auglaize and Maumee Rivers.

No one had any doubt that eventually Wayne would launch a massive campaign against the tribes, but, still buoyed by the victory over St. Clair, the Indians considered themselves virtually indomitable. This confidence was shaken and the Indian forces deeply shocked when their champion, Michikiniqua — Little Turtle — refused to lead them in the inevitable battle against Wayne. They bitterly accused him of cowardice.

"We have beaten the enemy twice under separate commanders," he replied seriously, "but hear me! We cannot expect the same good fortune always. The Americans are now led by a chief who never sleeps. The night and day are alike to him and during all the time that he has been marching on our villages, notwithstanding the watchfulness of our young men, we have never been able to surprise him. There is something whispers to me that it would be prudent to listen to his offers of peace."

The chiefs would not have it and they contemptuously deposed him, naming Blue Jacket as their sole commander. But things did not go too well. Blue Jacket assembled a thousand warriors at the mouth of the Auglaize and marched them against Fort Recovery, where a hard battle was fought. The Indians killed fifty Americans and took three hundred horses, yet their cries of victory were subdued. Every warrior knew beyond doubt that they should have taken the place by storm with virtually no loss to themselves, as Blue Jacket had said. That had not occurred, and their confidence was shaken.

Part of the reason why General Wayne was so capable in anticipating and thwarting the Indians was that he had taken on William Wells as his chief scout and spy, allowing the former adopted Miami to build up a spy company of his own choosing and then having the good sense to follow the recommendations these spies made. Throughout the winter of 1793 and into the spring and summer of this year the preparations by Wayne continued, and he gradually moved deeper into the Indian territory. At the confluence of the St. Joseph and St. Marys River, where Harmar's army had burned Miamitown and Hardin had taken the little girl named Pskipahcah Ouiskelotha into his custody, Wayne's army built a very substantial installation and named it Fort Wayne after their commander. This was followed by the construction of another fort at the mouth of the Auglaize where it emptied into the Maumee, and it was named Fort Defiance.

Finally, Wayne was ready. Taking advantage of the advice and intelligence provided him by Wells and his company of spies, Wayne launched his major attack against the Indians on August 20 at a place called Fallen Timbers, near the rapids of the Maumee. It was a resounding defeat for Blue Jacket's forces. Many Indians were killed, including Sauwaseekau, one of the triplets. Those who survived the initial attack retreated the short distance to the British Fort Miami. Spemica Lawba recalled only too well the dreadful bitterness in the words of Tecumseh as he had related what happened then.

"We asked them for the help they had promised for so long; asked them to send out their soldiers and artillery to help drive back the enemy. But they looked down at us over the walls of the fort like frightened birds and told us to go away, that they could not help us."

The defeat was of such magnitude and so shattering to the Indians that the chiefs sued for peace and a delegation of them met with General Wayne. He advised them to go back to their villages and remain quiet throughout the winter and then for all the chiefs and their delegations to assemble at Fort Greenville the following June to negotiate a peace treaty that would end the wars between Americans and Indians for all time. But rumors of what some of the terms of this treaty would be leaked out, and Tecumseh and many others were appalled.

"By signing such a treaty," Tecumseh declared with cold fury at the first Shawnee council following the defeat, "we will sign away all that is of value to us."

Catahecassa argued that it was the only sensible course and that while certainly the Indians would have to make concessions, they would still have their lives. Furthermore, their families would be safe from the spectre of death.

"Better that we leave our bones to bleach in the sun on these lands and know that we have died with honor, dignity and self-respect intact," Tecumseh responded, "than to live without them under the heel of such an enemy!"

Thus had begun a series of tribal councils marked by serious disputes between them that fomented a rift in the tribe. It was clear that many members of the tribe felt as Tecumseh did. But there were even more who were tired of years of war and strife and yearned for peace, and these sided with Catahecassa.

Abruptly Spemica Lawba's reverie was broken and he was snapped back to the present as Catahecassa again took the floor and raised his arms for silence. The heavy murmuring stilled and Catahecassa looked out across them, his face set in grim lines. His gaze stopped as it fell on Tecumseh and his words were flat.

"You are not a chief, Tecumseh," he said, "much less the principal chief of this tribe; nor, by its laws and traditions, can you ever become such a chief. You attempt to take onto yourself powers that are not rightfully yours, and I will not have it. As I have said, we have no choice in the matter. When the general-who-never-sleeps holds his council in the summer to come, I will be there and I will sign it on behalf of *all* the Shawnees, including you, Tecumseh."

"Not including me," said Tecumseh coldly, coming to his feet, "for if this is the will of the Shawnees, then I can no longer be a Shawnee."

There was a gasp at his words, and Spemica Lawba was stunned. His beloved uncle was voluntarily exiling himself from the tribe — something no one else in the tribe's history had ever done. He watched unbelievingly as Tecumseh strode to the doorway of the council house and paused there. Wasegoboah abruptly came to his feet and joined him, followed by Lowawluwaysica and Kumskaka and perhaps two score others. Tecumseh let his gaze pass over those who remained seated, including Blue Jacket, until he came to Spemica Lawba. He looked at his nephew for a long moment, then turned and vanished outside, followed by those who had joined him.

For the first time in his life, Spemica Lawba strongly disagreed with his uncle. Catahecassa was their chief, whose direction all Shawnees were bound by the traditions of the tribe to follow. But even apart from tradition, Spemica Lawba knew he would follow the course Catahecassa had chosen, for he truly believed it was the only course that could result in peace for the tribe.

Despite his conviction, Spemica Lawba was devastated.

CHAPTER XIII

August 22, 1795

PEMICA LAWBA rode his horse quietly, no more than a mile or so now from his own wegiwa in Wapatomica. He was wondering — as he had wondered a hundred times or more during this summer — if the course he had chosen was correct. It was not something anyone could tell him; the answer could be found only in his own heart.

So difficult, he thought, to be torn inside regarding where one's loyalty lay. Should it be predicated on love? On responsibility? On tradition? On duty? Should it be something that one knew instinctively? Or should it be a combination of all these things? He shook his head. The answer would not come easily. Perhaps one simply made a choice, as he had done, in the direction toward which he was most inclined and then stuck to it and had faith that he had chosen correctly. Yes, that had to be it — faith. Faith and hope. Nevertheless, the doubts still assailed him and he was troubled.

He had hoped, when Tecumseh and his other two uncles and his stepfather had walked out on the final council with Catahecassa last winter, that somehow there would come a reconciliation and the matter could be settled without permanent rift. It hadn't happened that way. When spring had come, Tecumseh and those who had elected to follow him — either through loyalty to him or through their own similar conviction that what was occurring was wholly wrong and would leave them without honor or dignity or in a land populated by whites — left the tribe and established a new village of their own on Deer Creek, some thirty or forty miles southeast. It was a wrenching time for Spemica Lawba, for not only had his three uncles and step-father gone, but his mother, Tecumapese, had gone as well. And they were upset when he would not accompany them.

"Please, Spemica Lawba," his mother had begged, "come with us. Tecumseh is right. What has happened and what is going to happen is wrong and our people can only suffer for it in the end."

Spemica Lawba had shaken his head sadly. "I cannot, Mother. I must go the way our chief says, not merely because he is our chief, but because it is what *I* believe as well. For years I have yearned for events to occur that would lead to our people living in peace and harmony with the whites. Now that is coming to pass and I cannot turn my back on it. You and Tecumseh and the others believe we will suffer for it in the end, but I believe, as does Catahecassa and those who remain here, that the lot of the Shawnees will be improved by it and for the first time in the memory of many of us — perhaps all! — we will be able to live in peace. No more fear of armies sweeping into our villages to kill and destroy. That alone is worth a great deal."

And so they had gone away and something had gone out of the spirit of the Shawnees who remained. There were many — Blue Jacket among them — who still entertained doubts, and councils continued to be held. Twelve tribes had been invited by General Wayne to participate in the great peace conference to be initiated at Greenville the first of June, and yet the Shawnees, embroiled in their continuing councils, though they were closest to Greenville, were the last tribal delegation to appear.

The peace treaty talks officially began on June 15 but it was not until July 31 that Catahecassa arrived with his delegation, which included Black Snake and Blue Jacket as well as Spemica

Lawba. And in order for the treaty talks to begin in an atmosphere free of animosity, Wayne ordered an unequivocal prisoner exchange: all Americans who were holding Indians prisoner had to give them back to their people; similarly, all whites being held prisoner by Indians had to be released. Both sides agreed to this as the first matter of business, and immediately messengers had been sent out with orders from General Wayne and the principal chiefs for this prisoner exchange to begin quickly. It would take a while, but it would be accomplished.

Tecumseh and his followers refused to attend the treaty talks.

Because of his skill in the English language, Spemica Lawba was taken by the former Miami, William Wells, and personally introduced as Johnny Logan to General Wayne and the officer's principal aide, William Henry Harrison. The young Shawnee made a strongly favorable impression on both, and at once he had been hired to serve as an interpreter during the talks. This not only increased his prestige among his own people, it filled him with a sense of gratification: at last he was actively doing something to help his people and perhaps to bring reality to the dream he had harbored for so long.

The long involved talks had been an education for him and so well did he serve, William Henry Harrison suggested that when it was all over, there were perhaps other jobs in Indian-American relations in which Johnny Logan might be a valuable asset to both his own people and the Americans. Spemica Lawba indicated a keen interest.

On August 10, the Greenville Treaty had been signed. As a parting gift, the chiefs who had participated were given brass medallions as symbols of lasting friendship between the races. By that time many of the captives who had been held by both sides, sometimes for years, had been returned to their people and others were still being released.

It took a few days following the conclusion of the Greenville Treaty for matters to be wrapped up and the parties involved to head home. But there was one group of five which did not set

out for home at once. It included Blue Jacket, Shemeneto —
Black Snake — and Spemica Lawba of the Shawnees, along with
a burly chief of the Potawatomi named Chaubenee, who had
been born an Ottawa but who had married into the Potawatomi
tribe, and was now one of their chiefs, and a young half-breed
named Sauganash, whose mother was a Potawatomi and whose
father was a British officer and trader. This group headed for
Tecumseh's Deer Creek village to tell him the details of the strong
treaty that had been signed.

Tecumseh ordered that their horses be taken care of, provided
them with food, and, afterwards, sat and smoked pipes and talked
with them. They were joined by Tecumapese, Wasegoboah,
Kumskaka, Lowawluwaysica — whose one good eye glared angrily at Spemica Lawba, whom he considered a traitor to the
family — and a Wyandot chief named Roundhead, who was a
strong ally of Tecumseh and believed as he did that there could
never be peace with honor between Indians and Americans.

Tecumseh and his followers listened as his visitors related the
details of the Greenville Treaty proceedings. A permanent peace
was theirs at last, they said. Tecumseh's expression had turned
melancholy, however, and he shook his head.

"You have the peace you wanted," he told them, "but at what
price? In exchange for that peace, you have given the Americans
what they wanted — half of the entire Ohio Country, plus six-
teen large tracts of land deep in Indian territory where the
Americans are free to build new forts and use them as a toehold
for future acquisitions of Indian lands. The places where our
fathers and grandfathers lie in rest are now owned by the Americans. The places where we hunted and fished and where our
villages were, these places are now owned by the Americans.
This very village where we sit is, by the terms of that treaty
you have made, now on land owned by the Americans and we
are told that we must vacate. For such concessions you have
been guaranteed peace, but I tell you this: it is a peace that will
last only until the Americans fill that land they have gained with

themselves and begin reaching out for more. Then the troubles will start all over again. So it has been and so it will be, always, until there are no more Indians."

"For those concessions of land that were made, Tecumseh," Blue Jacket interjected softly, "we have received more than merely guarantees of peace. Each of the twelve tribes who signed the treaty received an equal payment and each will receive an annuity of goods."

"Eleven of the twelve tribes who signed the treaty," Tecumseh reminded bluntly, his voice sharpening, "lost nothing. None of their lands were taken. They were paid for lands belonging to the Shawnees. But even had the land belonged to them, look much more closely at what price was paid. You have told me that each of the twelve tribes received $1,666, plus an annuity amounting to $825. That is hardly a bargain of which to be proud, considering the vast extent of land sold to the whites. They have purchased *our* birthright for the sum of *one cent for every six acres* and a guarantee of peace which the Shemanese will adhere to only so long as it serves their purpose to do so."

"Uncle," spoke up Spemica Lawba earnestly, "what has been accomplished by this treaty cannot be judged on price alone. What price can be set on peace of mind? What price can be set on the knowledge that now we can leave our villages and when we return our homes will still be there, our families will still be safe and not killed or in captivity, our crops will still be growing in their fields or still safely stored to prevent famine among our people in the winter? What price can be set for the peace we have all yearned for so much?"

Tecumseh looked for a long quiet moment at his twenty-year-old nephew, and when at last he replied, there was pain and bitterness in the words. "The white man's cows and pigs live in peace . . . until he is ready to slaughter them." His gaze took in all his visitors. "You who have come here are convinced you have done the right thing. I truly hope you are correct and that I am wrong. But my heart tells me that such is not so. At this

time we who live in this village have, by your concessions, become trespassers." The bitterness increased. "My people and I
will remain here until our corn is harvested and then we will
move away."

"But to where, uncle?" Spemica Lawba asked, feeling Tecumseh's pain in his own heart. "Catahecassa cannot allow you
to return to our villages now. He said this would raise ill feelings and dissension among our people."

"Who cares what Catahecassa says now?" Lowawluwaysica
spat out. "He has proven himself unworthy, a tool of the
Sheman—"

"*Enough!*" Tecumseh cut him off with a slashing motion of his
hand. He seemed about to reprimand his young brother more,
but then changed his mind. His tone of voice was less bitter
when he continued speaking, but there was an implacability in
his words that was chilling. "I would not return to the villages
even were I welcome," he said softly, "because I could not live
with what is in my heart and mind and still abide by the leadership of Catahecassa. Our chief has been a good chief since the
death of Black Fish," he glanced briefly at Lowawluwaysica, "but
he is weary of war — as you are, nephew — and thinks he is
best serving our people by ceding lands instead of lives." He
shrugged. "Perhaps he is correct, but I cannot live with that.
This is — was — our land and the bones of our fathers and our
father's fathers are buried here. If we cannot protect what is
ours, what then is left to us? No, Spemica Lawba," he went on,
sadness returning to his voice, "I will not return to our villages.
I will return above the new treaty line on the Great Miami River,
but in a village of my own making, and perhaps not for long.

"Weh-yeh-pih-ehr-sehn-wah," he went on, turning his attention to Blue Jacket, "it has been good seeing you again. And
you, Chaubenee, and our new young friend, Sauganash. Though
the news has been painful, I thank you for bringing it." He
stood and walked to the doorway of the wegiwa, where he

paused, his back to them. Chief Roundhead, resplendent as always in fine garb, stirred, as if to speak, but then settled back when Tecumseh turned around to face them. His features were etched with grim lines and his voice laced with cold determination.

"Only this do I have left to say. My heart is a stone: heavy with sadness for my people; cold in the knowledge that no treaty will keep the whites out of our lands; hard with the determination to resist so long as I live and breathe. Now we are weak and many of our people are afraid. But hear me! I tell you now what I once told Spemica Lawba: a single twig breaks, but the bundle of twigs is strong. Someday I will embrace our brother tribes and draw them into a bundle and together we will win our country back from the Americans."

Blue Jacket studied him with a piercing stare and then finally nodded. "I think maybe you will," he said.

Now Spemica Lawba, astride his horse, saw Wapatomica in the distance ahead and pushed aside the memories of that meeting two days ago which continued to weigh so heavily in his heart. He kicked his heels to the horse's side and completed the ride into the village at a brisk canter. He found himself just in time to meet an American major who had arrived for a twofold purpose. His name was Thomas Hardin and he had come to deliver up to Catahecassa certain Shawnees who had been prisoners in Kentucky, many for long periods. He also brought a message from his father-in-law, Benjamin Logan, for Spemica Lawba. It was a simple message: "Tell my adopted son, Johnny Logan, that his adopted father misses him and loves him and hopes one day we will meet again."

Spemica Lawba felt a rush of warmth upon hearing the message and immediately dictated a similar one of his own for Hardin to relay back: "Tell my adopted father, Benjamin Logan, that his adopted son, Johnny, misses him as well, loves him as well, and also wishes for our reunion some time. And tell him equally that Johnny Logan has lived up to the promises he made on their last day together, and that he will continue to honor them."

Hardin nodded. "May I call you Johnny?" he asked. At Spemica Lawba's nod he went on. "For myself, Johnny, I would like to ask a favor of you. Among the Shawnees I have brought here today is one who has not been a captive in that sense of the word. My father found her in a wegiwa near Miamitown five years ago when he was with General Harmar. He brought her home and adopted her into our family. Now she is like a sister to me and I am concerned for her welfare. I would like to ask, if you are of a mind to do so, Johnny, that you will occasionally stop to see her and make sure she is safe and happy. Her name is Pskipahcah Ouiskelotha. Her parents are dead and she will undoubtedly be taken into the household of the only living blood relative she has, her uncle, even though she did not know him well. He is her father's brother, a warrior named Tornado."

"I knew him," Spemica Lawba said quickly. "He is dead. He was one of those who was killed at Fallen Timbers."

"That is sad," Hardin said. "I am sorry. The news will grieve her. Now I don't know what to say except ask if you will help her and care for her."

"Of course I will," said the Shawnee without hesitation.

Hardin smiled and shook his hand, then led him to where the prisoners were being welcomed by a large group of the villagers. One of the newly returned stood somewhat apart from the others, her back to them, as they approached.

"Bluebird?" Hardin said.

The sixteen-year-old girl turned, her smile for him strained.

"This is Johnny Logan," the young officer said. "Among your people he is known as Spemica Lawba. As you know, he became the adopted son of my father-in-law many years ago, much as you became the adopted daughter of my father. And as you are being returned to your people now, so he was returned. I'm sorry to tell you this, Bluebird, but your uncle, Tornado, is no longer living." There was an immediate look of consternation in her eyes and her lower lip began to tremble. Her adopted brother put his arm about her shoulder and held her close to him. "Don't be afraid, Bluebird," he said gently. "Johnny has agreed to help. He will take care of you — protect you. Won't you, Johnny?"

Spemica Lawba nodded, but he could not speak. Bluebird was the most beautiful thing he had ever seen and abruptly his blood was racing. He felt dizzy, lightheaded. He reached out and touched her arm with his fingertips. Their eyes met fully for the first time, and she smiled faintly at him.

In that moment, Spemica Lawba knew he was in love with Pskipahcah Ouiskelotha.

CHAPTER XIV

October 30, 1795

ROM THE first moment he saw her, there was no doubt in the mind of Spemica Lawba that Pskipahcah Ouiskelotha would become his wife. She was tall and willowy, uncommonly graceful in her movements, quick to laughter and almost never moody, though she was a very sensitive person. Her features were smoothly chiseled and her beauty was enhanced by deep, dark, intelligent eyes framed by high cheekbones. Her hair, long and sleek, so black that it had a distinct bluish sheen to it in certain light, was usually worn in a single long braid, though occasionally allowed to fall free to mid-waist.

Though Spemica Lawba had taken her into his own wegiwa, their relationship was still one of unattached individuals, not mates, with no sexual familiarity occurring between them. She slept in her own bed in a compartment divided by slung blankets from the rest of the wegiwa, although they shared their meals at the central fire in the wegiwa. It was obvious that she was no less smitten with him than he was with her, and they spent endless hours together talking, sharing their experiences of childhood and captivity, delighted that, if they chose, they could speak to one another in English as well as in the Shawnee tongue.

It was at the end of their first two months together that an unexpected but perfect opportunity presented itself for them to become husband and wife.

Ever since the return of a great many Shawnees to their own people from captivity, according to the terms of the Greenville Treaty, there had been a period of readjustment. Many who returned found that their husbands or wives had died or been killed during their absence. Similarly, many men and women of the tribe who believed their wives or husbands were among the captured and would be returned, discovered to their dismay that the loved one had long ago died or been killed. Because of this, much disruption was occurring, and those whose family lives had always been secure found themselves unattached, drifting and needful of a spouse.

The family was an extremely important facet of Shawnee life. It was, in large measure, the foundation of their strength, and therefore the situation existing now, where so many had lost their mates, was undesirable and threatening to the stability of the nation. In an effort to resolve this matter, Chief Catahecassa, soon after the final prisoner exchange had been made, proclaimed that this year's Harvest Moon would also be the Nuptial Moon. There was much excitement at this announcement. Long ago in Shawnee history the Nuptial Moon had been a traditional affair occurring annually, but the custom had begun to die out about a century ago. In the past half-century the Nuptial Moon had been proclaimed only three times, and so the fact that it was to occur again was not only cause for excitement, it also served to imbue the Shawnees with the feeling that stability was returning to their existence. The rite was to occur in all the Shawnee villages simultaneously, but it would be most dramatic in the capital village of the Shawnee nation, Wapatomica. Extensive preparations for the great feast were begun at once and consumed almost every waking moment until the time of the Nuptial Moon was at hand.

The festivities began when one of the village subchiefs, appointed by Catahecassa to the honor, began walking through the

Wapatomica at sunset, pausing outside the doorway of each wegiwa to make his loud chanting proclamation. It was a proclamation comprised of three pertinent statements:

"*Pay heed!*

"*All inside are no longer bound to one another by vows.*

"*All inside who were married are no longer married.*

"*All marriages in this household are now dissolved.*"

It took until the last vestiges of dusk for the crier's chant to be completed at each wegiwa. At that moment there were, by Shawnee law, no longer any valid marriages remaining in the tribe. Only then was a great fire built in the midst of the expansive open area before the *msi-kah-mi-qui* and all residents of the village collected here, some bringing previously prepared food and drink, others bringing prepared raw flesh — deer, bear, turkey, quail, grouse, squirrel, rabbit, raccoon, dog, fish, goose, duck, opossum and many others. Some of these were to be cooked at the fire on spits, some would be wrapped in wet cornhusks and baked on hot coals, some to be placed directly on the glowing coals to be broiled until black on the outside and juicy pale pink inside. Most of the meat, however, was cut into chunks rich with fat and, along with a variety of vegetables — corn, beans, peas, turnips, potatoes, squash, onions and garlic — tossed into enormous black iron kettles to be cooked into a marvelously savory stew.

During the preparation period for the feast, great quantities of dried corn had been pounded in mortars made of upright sections of hollowed-out tree trunk until ground into extremely fine powder and then moistened and beaten and kneaded in loaves. These, also, were wrapped in layers of damp cornhusk and placed on pot-lids on the coals to bake, soon filling the air with tantalizing aroma. This was the basic bread, called *taquana.*

Pots of water were placed on the coals to come to a boil for the preparation of another kind of pastry called *skepulhawna* — blue biscuit — which was a sort of dumpling. The same finely ground corn flour was used, to which was added pure white ashes from buckskin pouches. The ashes had been obtained by burning matured, well-dried beanhusks on flat rocks. Though the ashes were white when mixed with the corn flour, as water was added the dough that resulted was a very deep blue. When of exactly the right consistency, this dough was molded by hand into three-cornered biscuits to be dropped into the boiling water. *Skepulhawna* retained its pleasing deep-blue color when cooked and had a very delightful, unusually distinctive flavor. Large numbers were to be cooked simultaneously, since those left over could be dried and kept over long periods for future use, being reboiled when needed.

In baskets woven of cattail reeds there were immense quantities of sun-dried fruits — grapes, plums, dew-berries, strawberries, cherries, blackberries, persimmons and pawpaws — to be eaten as they were, along with a variety of nuts — shelled black walnuts and hickory nuts, acorn-like hazel nuts and tiny triangular beechnuts that had already been roasted. In some cases during the preparation period, the dried fruits had been softened by lengthy immersion in a heavy liquid of maple sugar and water, then kneaded into the dough and baked in flat loaves that were very dense, sweet, and studded with the fruit particles and nuts. Especially favored was a pastry of this sort called *muchahseeminitakuwha*, in which dried persimmon was the only fruit used. The resultant cake had a sweet yet puckery taste.

A small quantity of liquor on hand, obtained from British traders, was mixed with a sort of beer the Shawnees made called *darmi*. The beverage, contained in dried and hollowed-out longneck gourds, was only very mildly intoxicating, but very flavorful. In addition, there were numerous containers of a thin, sweet, maple-sugar drink called *marlsi-napi*.

At last the Nuptial Moon festivities began, and in a short time the calm night air was filled with a multitude of wonderful aromas. Well before midnight the feasting began. The initial repast lasted for several hours and then the dancing commenced, continuing throughout the remainder of the night. The men — about a hundred at a time — danced by themselves first, then the women, in similar numbers, by themselves. Each group started out dancing in a long line, one behind the other, swaying and shuffling, leaping high and stamping their bare feet as strings of bells tied around their ankles tinkled rhythmically. All this was accompanied by the throbbing of heavy drums, the higher-pitched staccato pulsing of tom-toms and rattling of gourds partially filled with pebbles or dried beans. Overriding it all were the rising and falling melodic cries of a chanter. It was a very wild, very primitive breathtaking spectacle. In succession, the line of dancers snaked itself into the form of a moving square, then into a circle and, finally, into a figure-eight formation.

The men danced past the rows of women and each woman who cared to do so reached out and touched the man of her choice as he gyrated past. More often than not, those whose marriages had just been dissolved touched their former husbands, but this was not required and there were those who selected other than the previous mate. Those who were fifteen summers or older and had never been married touched whomever they chose . . . or no one. At such a touch, the man dancing would erupt in a loud high-pitched shriek and stamp his feet for many seconds as he moved off. When the men completed one full revolution of their dance sequences, they moved off and seated themselves and the women began theirs. The same basic steps and formations were enacted, this time with the men selecting. If the man touched the woman who had touched him, the two danced off together to the end of the line and then the dancing for these two ceased. During the remainder of the festivities they would participate only in the singing and feasting.

Time after time the lines were formed and danced, broke apart and then reformed and danced again. For three days and nights — with those who became exhausted sleeping whenever or wherever they chose — the ritual was continued. Toward the end there were only a small number of dancers left, largely those who had no wish to be married and so made no choice or those who had made choices but the proposed mate had not returned the touch.

For those who had never been married before — Spemica Lawba and Pskipahcah Ouiskelotha among them — it was customary to dance without signifying a choice until the third night. When that time came, the lovely Shawnee girl reached out and touched Spemica Lawba's arm as he whirled past and he had grinned broadly and screeched a triumphant cry, as many others were doing periodically. And when, in turn, Pskipahcah Ouiskelotha danced past, her hair swaying and swishing behind as if comprised of strands of finest silk, he touched her and instantly a glad cry sprang to her lips. On the next round, as Spemica Lawba passed, Pskipahcah Ouiskelotha leaped to her feet and took hold of the blanket he had draped across his shoulders. Gripping it tightly, she danced with him to the end of the line, where both fell out.

They sat together after that, talking and eating, as others were doing with their chosen mates, until sunrise of the fourth day. At that time all the music and dancing ceased except for the rhythmic throbbing of one large drum. In time to its beat the couple walked hand in hand to Spemica Lawba's wegiwa. They paused outside the doorway and there, in time to the drumbeat, each chanted his own part of the responsive litany both had learned as little children but had never before used.

It was he who chanted first:

"My wegiwa door is open wide,
"Alone for you my love; alone for you my bride."

Her response was immediate:

"I come! I come! My heart is won!
"The sun is up; I give my love to you."

He replied:

"The sun shines bright with morning light
"Upon my bride . . . my bride and me."

She faced him directly and her voice dropped to only a whisper:

"I give my heart, my hand, my vow,
"To serve and care for you."

They embraced for a quiet moment, then pulled apart and with hands joined, chanted in unison the final lines of the litany:

"Moneto, guide us on our way, throughout our lives;
"The sun is up! The sunrise lights our wedding day!"

Hands still clasped, they entered the door of the wegiwa, closing the flap of hide behind them, alone together at last in a new and wonderful way.

Spemica Lawba and Pskipahcah Lawba were husband and wife.

CHAPTER XV

May 8, 1798

O N HIS WAY to this place, this tiny village on the Whitewater River in the Indiana Territory, Spemica Lawba wondered if it were wise for him to make this visit; wondered if word of how he had been employed for over a year had reached Tecumseh; wondered if Tecumapese was angry because he had never presented the woman her son had married, the woman who had borne the grandson she had never seen. He wondered if his uncles and stepfather bore a grudge against him because he had chosen to remain with the tribe. And he wondered if this was not all a huge mistake, coming to see them again. Whether or not it was, there had been no choice. There was no one better suited than he for the mission Catahecassa had delegated to him.

So now he was here, and there had been embraces, friendly greetings, friendly words. They had eaten together and smoked together and no discord had been struck. He tried to convince himself that none would be, but in his heart he knew better. Common politeness — whether to stranger or family member — dictated that no business be broached, no critical word spoken, until bellies were filled, until pipes were smoked.

Spemica Lawba sitting in his uncle's lodge on a high bank above the Whitewater, looked across the fire at him. Tecumseh had changed a great deal since his nephew had seen him last, over two years before. He was still a striking individual and the similarity in the physical appearance of nephew and uncle was still very apparent. But, at thirty summers, the quality of boyishness that had always been a part of Tecumseh was gone, replaced by a quiet manly strength. Sorrows and disappointments had begun to etch lines of character on his face, his gaze was more penetrating than ever before, the jut of his chin more firm, his whole carriage of greater self-assurance. That entire effect was considerably heightened now by the firelight flickering before him.

Kumskaka and Lowawluwaysica sat to Tecumseh's left and Spemica Lawba's mother, Tecumapese, sat to her brother's right, with Wasegoboah beside her. Despite the qualms suffered while en route here, Spemica Lawba found the reunion a happy moment. It was seemingly the same for the others as well. Over their meal they had talked only in pleasantries of many things common in their pasts and things of no great consequence that they had done individually since last they met. But, finally, the dinner finished and the pipes smoked, it was time, as all present knew, for Spemica Lawba to state his purpose in coming.

Tecumseh opened the door for that conversation. "My heart wants to believe," he said slowly, a touch of wistfulness in his voice, "that you have come to join us, but my mind says this is not so and that you wish only for us to return to Wapatomica with you and live again under Catahecassa."

Spemica Lawba shifted uneasily as he grunted an assent. "As always," he added, "your mind sees the truth. It has been two years since the Greenville Treaty was signed and Catahecassa points with pride to the fact that what he said would be has come to pass. It has been a good and lasting treaty, with no indication that it will be broken. Because of this, I have been sent by our chief to ask that you and those who follow you return to your people."

"Catahecassa is *your* chief, nephew!" Lowawluwaysica had

spoken up harshly, the deeply shadowed empty eyesocket and his unpleasant features combining in a malevolent mask. "He is no longer *ours!* We are no longer Shawnees. We —"

Tecumseh's abruptly raised hand cut him off. With tightened lips, the elder uncle turned back to Spemica Lawba. "The words of your uncle Lowawluwaysica are sharply spoken," he said, "but they are nevertheless true. You know that all of us here — and those others who have followed us — cannot agree with Catahecassa that the Greenville Treaty is binding upon us all and that we must bury the hatchet forever. I had always respected Catahecassa, always admired him, and so it came as a hard blow to learn that he believed — *still* believes, in fact, contrary to the evidence — that the Shemanese will live up to that agreement. It is why we drifted apart. It is why others clung to me who felt as I did, that our troubles with the Shemanese are not ended. Now the Americans have enforced that measure of their treaty drawn with the British long ago which said that the British must surrender Detroit to them, as well as the post where the great lakes meet in the north, Fort Mackinac. Now the Shemanese soldiers occupy these places and, bit by bit, as I said they would do, they slip into our lands and nibble at them. They want ever more what is ours, while our continued wish is to have returned to us that of ours which the Shemanese have already taken."

He paused, staring into the dwindling flames, but no one spoke. After a moment he continued in a level voice, but with an edge of bitterness underlying his words. "How does one come to agreement with they who have burned our villages, killed or imprisoned our people, driven us off our ancestral lands, and," he stared particularly hard at Spemica Lawba now, "driven wedges among us to divide us? How does one come to agreement with they who sit at this moment on lands stolen from us? We cannot. We step aside now because we are weak, but such will not always be. One day we will be in a position to negotiate from strength, not from weakness, and when that time comes we will rightfully reclaim that which was taken away."

He lapsed into silence again and this time for so long that Spemica was on the verge of replying when his mother spoke up. Her words were uttered softly, but there was a great sadness in her voice. "Tecumseh does not always speak what is in his heart, my son," she said, "if he feels it serves no good purpose. But since I am your mother, I will speak the words he has left unsaid."

Spemica Lawba nodded, but his stomach muscles tightened as she continued.

"When you married Pskipahcah Ouiskelotha, your bride should have been given the opportunity to come to know the family to which you belong. You have denied her — and us! —this right. When your son, Outhowwa Skishequih" — Yellow Eye — "was born, it should have been close to his grandmother and his great-uncles, whose blood also runs in his veins. Yet, they have never seen him. Your second child will be born at the end of the Heat Moon. Will we also be deprived of seeing this one?"

Spemica Lawba was surprised that they even knew of his son's birth over a year ago, much less the present pregnancy of his wife. With a sinking sensation, he was sure now that they knew much more and in that surmise he was only too correct.

"It is," Tecumapese continued, "a difficult enough burden to bear for me — for us! — to know that you have chosen to remain with Catahecassa on the Maumeetheepi rather than with us, who are your first blood. It is much worse, much more difficult to understand, when little birds whisper in our ears that you serve with and for the Shemanese; that you carry the words of the soldier Harrison at Fort Washington as his messenger."

"And," put in Kumskaka scornfully, "that you answer to him and others under the Shemanese name of Johnny Logan."

"It is hard, as well," his mother continued, silencing her younger brother with a raised eyebrow, "to understand why you have become the friend of the one who was raised as Apekonit, the son of Michikiniqua, who renounced the Miamis and resumed his white identity as William Wells and who now aids the Shemanese as a spy for them. All these things are true."

It was not a question, but Spemica Lawba nodded, eyes downcast. In a moment he raised his head and met her gaze, his inner misery evident. But there was defiance there as well. "It is true, Mother," he said, "but not *all* of the Shemanese are bad. Many, such as he who gave me the name of Johnny Logan, are good men who wish for nothing to which they are not entitled."

He transferred his gaze to Tecumseh. "See what has happened to us. Once we were so strong that the Shemanese begged us for favors. Now, while they have increased to a strength we never knew, we have weakened steadily. More than half our people are separated and live now far west of the Missitheepi. Those who remain see the choices they have only too clearly: oppose the Shemanese and die . . . to no purpose; or else accept the terms of the agreement we have made with them, even though they may not be the best for us, and live with them, accepting what little there is for us to accept, rather than to lose everything. *That* is what Catahecassa has asked me to express to you." His tone became imploring. "Tecumseh, for your sake and for the sake of our tribe which needs your strength and wisdom, come back to us."

Tecumseh shook his head. "It is not possible, Spemica Lawba," he said gently. "We are where we are."

"Then let me speak for myself rather than for Catahecassa," the younger man persisted. "Let me speak as one who loves you — as I do! — and wishes you only what is in your own best interest. Do not think it is through ignorance that I ask you to alter your stand. It is because I feel — I *know!* — that with your great leadership abilities, you might be able to bring to our people, through cooperation with the whites, what you now feel can only be gained through resistance."

He paused and was gratified to note that Tecumseh was exhibiting no impatience. His uncle was listening to him closely, obviously weighing the words and thoughts as they were expressed. Spemica Lawba prayed silently, briefly, to Moneto to give him the words he so desperately needed now.

"You feel," he went on, "that with such cooperation must come degredation, loss of self respect and dignity and, equally important, loss of our traditional lands. You wonder how, if this is true, I can support them, believe in them. I will tell you how: I have lived with these people, Tecumseh. I have seen what they have that we have not. I have seen their children sent to schools to learn of things far beyond the abilities of one's own parents to teach. I have seen the food they eat and the improved means by which they cook it; the fine homes in which they live in comfort. I have seen how their medicine keeps them healthy because it is based on knowledge rather than superstition. I have seen how they grow things — how they tend the earth with better tools and better seeds so that, with far less work, they produce more and better food for their people. I have seen how they have bred animals to provide more and better meat for their tables, so that they do not have to expend great energy in hunting wild game. And, Tecumseh, I have seen their love for one another, and their sorrow when a loved one is lost. These are love and grief which equal our own, despite our inclination to believe they have no feelings. And I have seen how their laws work to protect the innocent and punish those who do wrong.

"Tecumseh," he pleaded, "I know there are bad things about the whites, but so too are there bad things about our people. These we must live with and try to change for the better, no matter who we are or where we live. But you — you have the power to bring our people to a better future. You speak of dignity and self respect. Where is the dignity in gradual destruction? Where is the self respect in seeing one's own people hurt and hungry and cold, with nothing better in the future?"

He stopped again, drained by his own intense outpouring, but then went on, his voice softening and becoming even more compelling.

"It can be that none of those sad things need come to pass, if only we work with the whites. Not *for* them, Tecumseh, but *with* them, as partners in an effort to improve the lives of *all* people, Indian or white." He licked his lips, feeling he was talking in circles and suddenly not knowing what to say next. Tecumseh nudged him.

"And what of our lands, Spemica Lawba? Lands which you must know will be eaten up if we follow the course you advise."

"And what *of* our lands, Tecumseh?" Spemica Lawba threw the question back at him. "Is it not possible, uncle, that much of our trouble stems from our placing an unreasonably high value on them? Cannot *all* men use them? Of what value are they if holding them becomes nothing more than a reason for war and a place in which to leave our bones?"

Tecumseh came to his feet and moved around the fire until he was close to his nephew, who had risen to face him. Tecumseh placed his hand on his nephew's forearm and his smile was wistful.

"You are so young, Spemica Lawba. Your will is good, but your heart sees through eyes that have become clouded. I have known the whites well, too. I have seen some of their goodness, but far more of their bad. To all you have said I can only repeat what I said before. It is not possible. We are where we are. Our course is set and there is no turning back. By ourselves we cannot hope to recover what we have lost — what others have lost and are still losing. Now many of those others are beginning to feel the blade that has pierced us for so long. Some are beginning to listen with their heads instead of merely with their hearts. Soon many others will do so, also. When they do, then we will begin to have the *strength* to talk with the Shemanese."

"So you will remain here until then?"

Again Tecumseh shook his head. "No. This has only been a temporary stopping place for us. We have been asked by Buckangehela, chief of the Delawares, to come and reside among his people to the north of here on the Wuhkernekahtheepi" — White

River. "They have opened their hearts and arms to us without wishing to change how we believe, as our own Shawnees will not. They ask us to come and live with them, hunt with them, reside in peace with them. They have asked us, should the time come when it would be necessary, if we will lead them against any enemy who might threaten them. We have told them that we will."

With the utterance of those words, Spemica Lawba knew his fears were confirmed. There would never again be agreement between his uncle and his chief unless it was the Shawnee principal chief who changed his mind.

CHAPTER XVI

January 1, 1801

I N THE TWO and a half years that had passed since his final meeting with his mother and Tecumseh and the others, Spemica Lawba had changed considerably. At age twenty-six he had become a solid, serious man with direct gaze and remarkably sure reflexes. He was very intelligent and outwardly self-assured, but that latter aspect of his character was only a facade. Within his innermost heart and mind the doubts arose frequently to assail him.

Always before, he had been a happy, bright, engaging individual with a distinctly contagious grin. Nowadays, he seldom even smiled.

The doubts lay in the course he had chosen and whether or not he was right in pursuing it. Many times, as he rode alone on missions through woodlands or prairies, he spoke aloud to himself, setting himself up as two people who endlessly argued the relative merits and wisdom of his choice.

"It would be so easy," one part of his mind spoke aloud, "to return to my family and embrace them and their cause."

"Of course it would," the other part of his mind replied, "but since when has the correct course been the easier one?"

"Neither choice is easy!" he retorted.

"True. But going back would be easier."

"I never knew of Tecumseh making a choice based on how easy it might be."

"Well, then, what would Tecumseh do in my position?"

"He would do what is right."

"And what," that part of his mind mourned, "is right? And what is wrong?"

His mind shrugged. "There is one thing we *know* Tecumseh would do, given such choices. Only one."

"Which is?"

"He would strive to the last particle of his strength and intellect to help his people. So what are *you* doing?"

"I, too, am trying to help my people!" he flared at himself. "Look about us: the woods ring to the sound of white men's axes, just as the streams are dotted with their boats. The *Shemanese* are here to stay and to fight them is insanity. The *only* future for our people lies in accepting the whites and their ways and benefiting from the mixing of our races. That's where I may be of help. A concerned Indian close to the whites can be of immeasurable value in bringing this about."

"And that's what you are doing?"

"It is what I am *trying* to do. With Moneto's blessing — and God's — I will succeed."

"And you feel you are right?"

"I hope so. Yes! I *must* be right!"

"And if you are not?"

"I am!"

"But *if* you are not?"

A groan rumbled from his chest and he shook his head, trying to cast the troubling thoughts aside, but he could not. What if he *were* wrong? What if the choice he had made was the worst he could have made? What then?

"Then . . . then . . ." he concluded glumly to himself, ". . . I will have to finally admit it to myself and do what I can, in whatever position I then hold, to help my people. It is, I think, what Tecumseh would do."

And so it would go, time after time, his mind besieged and tormented. Yet, he had made his choice and in living up to it he was determined to become of great value to the whites as Johnny Logan. And he felt that in this way he would, one day, be of similar value to the Indians — as Spemica Lawba.

His prestige rose considerably when, as Johnny Logan, he was appointed as liaison and interpreter between the Americans and the Shawnees by the new Secretary of the Northwest Territory, William Henry Harrison. Along with William Wells, Johnny Logan served also as a spy, scout, guide and message carrier between the tribes and the government.

There was a mutual attraction between Johnny and Harrison and often the two talked together for long periods, discussing the respective problems of the whites and Indians in this area. The peace that Harrison had helped establish five and a half years ago with the Greenville Treaty was still in effect and seemed as strong as when signed, and Johnny was more than ever convinced that matters were on the right road and that eventually the knowledge, technology and freedom of the whites would be shared equally with the Indians. Harrison did nothing to disabuse him of his faith in these matters, but Harrison was nevertheless concerned. In the years since the treaty was signed, some forty-five thousand whites had settled in the Ohio Country and many more would be coming. The land cessions gained by the whites through that treaty, large as they were, clearly were not enough for the burgeoning white population. More land — Indian land — was needed for expansion and it was needed quickly.

Harrison, who was the most energetic, shrewd and ambitious white man Johnny Logan had ever met, had no great difficulty convincing his Shawnee aide that it would be of the greatest benefit to all the tribes to sell to the government whatever land it wanted. In this way, he assured Johnny, there would be increased settlement by whites and, as a result, increased benefits for the Indians through such contacts. The Indians would be exposed to cultural advances they had never had an opportunity for prior to now: they would be able to learn the white man's farming methods and mechanical skills; they would be able to learn how to raise livestock and therefore not have to depend on hunting skills and the vagaries of game populations to provide food for their families; they would eventually, Harrison assured him, be provided with schools in which they could learn to read and write and figure, where they could learn of art and science and a broad range of subjects that would raise their cultural foundation and expand their horizons.

It all sounded so wonderful to Spemica Lawba, precisely what he had envisoned for the Shawnees and other Indians for so long. And because of his enthusiasm to help bring about this goal, he considered the trading of extensive stretches of land by the Indians to accomplish this end a wholly worthwhile project.

In the visits to various tribes, upon which Harrison sent him as his emissary, Spemica Lawba extolled the benefits to be gained by the tribes in adopting the ways of the whites, in melding their cultures to the benefit of both. He pointed out the horrors that all the tribes had undergone throughout their histories — the perpetual wars with other tribes; the periodic famines that descended upon them and caused so much privation and death; the sicknesses that sprang up and raced through the tribes, killing scores, hundreds, even thousands of them; the gradually increasing difficulties encountered in the annual hunts, where game was less and less abundant; the incredible difficulty of their existence where simply the effort to survive cost them almost all their energies leaving no time or inclination to learn more about their world and to enjoy life.

His words had an impact on many of the Indians. There were those who turned their backs to him and considered him a traitor or a tool of the whites. But more and more, as he brought gifts to them from Harrison, along with promises of much more in the future, they were softening and beginning to wonder if perhaps Spemica Lawba was not, after all, correct in what he told them. None could deny that his sole aim seemed to be nothing more than improving the lot of his own people. And none could deny that for the first time in their history, many tribes were living without the threat of war overhanging them and it was a blessing of great significance. Even the Shawnee principal chief, Catahecassa, was very impressed with what Spemica Lawba was doing and very proud of him.

The fact that the first government-sponsored program to teach the Indians to farm using white man's methods — a program initiated among the Miamis and Potawatomies and aided by William Wells — had turned out to be a total failure, was largely overlooked by Catahecassa. The fact that many Indians had no desire to have their way of life changed was disregarded by Harrison. The fact that many Indians had no desire to see white men get control of even more of the Indian lands was considered insignificant by almost all the whites and far too many of the "tamed" Indians.

There was only one, among all the Indians, who clearly saw the ramifications of the land-acquisition program of the whites; only one who saw clearly that those who sold their lands to the whites and began adopting white man's ways were insidiously destroying themselves — becoming no longer Indians with proud tribal heritage, but rather a breed of people who were and always would be treated as less-than-white, as inferiors. There was only one who saw that Harrison continued a subtle program to promote agitation and jealousy between the tribes and in this way prevent them from becoming any sort of significant threat to the government in what was occurring.

That man was Tecumseh.

It was at this moment — at this very instant that the nineteenth century was beginning — that Tecumseh spoke of these matters in a very secret council to a small core of his staunchest followers. They were assembled in a wegiwa in a Delaware Indian village on the Wuhkernekahtheepi — White River — less than twenty-five miles west of Fort Greenville and only a few

miles inside the Indiana Territory from the Ohio border. The
night was very clear and bitterly cold, but the doorway to the
wegiwa had been sealed with a heavy flap of bison hide and the
interior was pleasantly warm for the six men and one woman
inside. Five of the seven were closely related to Spemica
Lawba — his mother and three uncles and stepfather. In addition to Tecumapese, Tecumseh, Lowawluwaysica, Kumskaka
and Wasegoboah, Chaubenee of the Potawatomies was there —
perhaps the most devoted of Tecumseh's followers — and
Roundhead of the Wyandots.

The fact that the one-eyed Lowawluwaysica was here was
something of a surprise, since he had, to all outer appearances,
moved back to Wapatomica and been reinstated as a Shawnee
by Catahecassa. Only he and the members of this select group
on hand tonight knew that he had been sent back by Tecumseh
to keep track of what was occurring in the Shawnee nation and
to let Tecumseh know immediately if Catahecassa or Spemica
Lawba or any others of the Shawnees should waver in their af-
filiation with Harrison specifically and the whites in general. If
such wavering occurred, then steps could be taken to convince
them to throw in their lot with Tecumseh. Thus far Lowawluwaysica had been unsuccessful, but Tecumseh felt that his
younger brother's reestablishment in the tribe could have future
benefit and he had urged Lowawluwaysica to continue in the
halfhearted efforts the one-eyed man had begun to become a
Shawnee medicine man. He had done so and was making some
headway, returning to the White River to report to Tecumseh
only when summoned, as he had been for this meeting.

Tecumseh had been speaking to them for the better part of an
hour already, and they listened to him with rapt attention. It
was not an oration, for he was not delivering a speech or lectur-
ing, but merely talking to them in a calm and reasonable way as
they all sat about the fire. Yet, it had not taken the six listeners
long to realize that what they were hearing would be very likely
to alter the remainder of their lives.

Already Tecumseh had touched upon the ominous occurrences of the past year that affected them and all other Indians, either directly or indirectly. Nine moons ago, in March, Connecticut had ceded its original colonial claim, called the Western Reserve Lands, to the United States government. These lands, along the southern edge of Lake Erie in the Ohio Territory, were still part of the upper half of Ohio guaranteed to the Indians by the Greenville Treaty. Yet, immediately the government had commenced surveying and laying out the lands to satisfy land bounty warrants issued to American soldiers who had fought in the Revolution. At that time the fledgling United States had not had the money to pay her soldiers and so had promised them land instead; a promise now being fulfilled. By the Green Moon — April — a thousand settlers had poured into the Western Reserve and claimed land by right of their bounty warrants. Forests were leveled to feed the sawmills that had been built to provide lumber for the construction of homes. Woodlands and prairies were bisected by a network of over seven hundred miles of road cut through virgin territory, and another American army installation — Fort Industry — had been built near the mouth of the Maumee.

All the country westward, from Ohio's western boundary to the Missitheepi, had been established as the Indian Territory — better known as Indiana — with its seat of government placed at Vincennes on the Wabash River. A governor was needed for this new territory, and appointed to this powerful post by President John Adams was the red-headed, twenty-seven-year-old William Henry Harrison.

Tecumseh's lips tightened as he spoke Harrison's name, for Tecumseh knew, as no one else yet fully realized, that Harrison was by far the greatest living threat to the Indians in America — a man to be wary of; a foe to respect and fear greatly; an enemy with powerful resources; an adversary whom they would one day have to face squarely.

"All during this past summer," Tecumseh continued, "and

into the fall and winter and even now, this Governor Harrison has been establishing himself at Vincennes, building a great house such as this land has never seen, from which he intends to run our lives — mine, yours, the lives of all Indians. He is aided by many, but three in particular who can do us great harm. One of these," he glanced at the man to his left, "is a village chief of your own Potawatomi tribe, Chaubenee. His name is Winnemac and his lips are always at the ear of Harrison. Harrison listens! When the governor was only a young soldier himself at Fallen Timbers he learned important lessons from General Wayne; learned to listen to — and heed! — the advice of those who have been more intimate with the enemy than he. In this he admits humility and in that humility there is great strength. Few leaders ever acquire such ability, but those who do can accomplish many things."

Chaubenee nodded. "I know Winnemac," he said, "though not well. I have *heard* more of him than I know of my own witness. I am told that he considers himself to be more than he is; that he craves power over all the Potawatomi."

"You said three could do us harm, brother," put in Kumskaka. "Who are the other two?"

"Another," Tecumseh said, "is he who was once white, then Indian, now white again; he whom we knew as Apekonit, or sometimes Epiconyare" — there was contempt in his voice as he spat out the word, for *Epiconyare* meant "brave and loyal" — "but who is now William Wells. He learned much from his adopted father, Michikiniqua, and from the Miamis, until he began to be afraid of their future and returned to the protection of the whites. He knows about us and our ways and now he, too, tells Harrison many things and performs many tasks for him which he pretends are for our benefit."

He paused again, and when he did not resume speaking, Tecumapese rolled her eyes toward him and spoke the words he seemed reluctant to utter. "And the third of those Harrison listens to who can bring us great harm," she said tonelessly, "is my son and your nephew, Spemica Lawba."

Tecumseh nodded. "Yes. Everything I have learned of him points in that direction. He is dangerous to us because he believes in the path he has chosen. In his sincerity he becomes convincing to other Indians."

"Spemica Lawba is very popular in Wapatomica, brother," Lowawluwaysica agreed. "In fact, he is popular among all the Shawnees now and very well known among them." His good eye squinted almost closed and his expression became uglier. "What he tells them does nothing to help us. He is a white-lover!"

Tecumseh shook his head, his expression sad. "Long ago, because of the kindness of one of the Shemanese, our nephew turned his heart toward them. Now, though his wegiwa remains in Wapatomica and his loyalty with Catahecassa and his heart with Pskipahcah Ouiskelotha and the two sons she has borne him, he journeys often to Vincennes. There, Governor Harrison has come to rely heavily on him for many things, among which is to continue convincing Catahecassa that he must keep the Shawnees quiet and in place. And because Spemica Lawba is convinced he is acting in his people's best interests, he does so.

"Harrison sees things far too clearly for one with eyes so young," he went on, "and his eyes are set on more distant things that will affect us all."

Roundhead spoke up for the first time. "Your eyes are just as clear, Tecumseh, and they see farther and deeper. If they did not, we would not be here this night. Since you came to this village you have been thinking, and before that you thought on the Whitewater River. Even before that, at Deer Creek, it is said that you thought deeply. All of these thoughts of yours have now come together and it is time for them to become words for our ears."

Tecumseh's smile for him was brief and he nodded. "Yes, it is time for my thoughts to become words. I have a plan that I have been shaping for many seasons, and that plan is now ready. What I have envisoned may take ten or twelve summers of great effort to bring about but, with the help of all of you here, I can do it. I *will* do so! Should my plan ripen into success — *and it must!* — the Shemanese will be driven back, not only across the Spaylaywitheepi, but even beyond the mountains which first greet the morning sun.

"Time after time it has been proven that given equal arms and equal numbers, there is no force of white men who can stand before us. But previous efforts of the Indians to oppose the whites have always before been flawed by one grave fault. Such Indian forces before, formed only of a single tribe, ultimately became too weak to stand against the numbers and arms of whites brought against them. When the Indians made efforts to band several tribes together to face the armies — as they did under such great chiefs as Pontiac and Thayendanegea and even Michikiniqua — they eventually failed because of friction in leadership. In the past the tribes had often warred among themselves, so that even when at peace, Mohawks did not wish to fight under an Ottawa leader, Wyandots did not wish to fight under a Shawnee leader, Delawares did not wish to fight under a Potawatomi leader. So it happened, always, and the confederacies fell apart because of their own tribal jealousies and often because of the hatreds that had existed between them for so long a time that most could not even remember when they began.

"These confederacies were doomed from the beginning, but that is not what I will make. I — and most of you here — are no longer members of a tribe. We have separated from our tribe and we are now only Indians. And that is what all the warriors must be, if we are to have the strength we need to force back our enemies. We must journey to the various tribes and convince them that if they are to survive, they must put aside their tribal designations and become merely Indians — brothers united for a common purpose against the greatest enemy in any of our histories. We will form a new village and it will not be a village of any one tribe or even of confederated tribes. It will be a village of *Indians!* We will not be Shawnees nor Potawatomies nor Wyandots nor Cherokees nor Sioux. We will be *Indians*, all of us! It will happen; but it will not happen quickly. Ten or twelve summers of very great effort will be required to bring it about, but I tell you again, it *will* happen. With some of the tribes we will have to move slowly, carefully, gaining their confidence, their respect, their willingness to follow for the common good. With other tribes it will go swiftly, with only a word or two needed for the war belts to begin circulating and tomahawks to be struck into the war posts."

Tecumseh's eyes glittered with the passion of his vision, and his listeners were entranced by his words as he went on.

"With the help of Moneto and the gifts he has given me — the abilities to see and speak and convince — I will ride far and visit many. I will take my time and convince the tribes of the necessity of joining together without hatred between them to gnaw at them and eventually destroy them. I will tell them these things in such a manner that they will stamp their feet and clap their hands and shout, and they will chafe at any delay in forming the union. One by one I will draw them together and interweave them into a single force of warriors from fifty or more different tribes. When at last we confront the whites, it will not be with just a few thousand warriors. No! It will be with a single unified body of *fifty thousand* warriors!

"With such a force," he went on after a momentary pause, "we may have no need greater than showing ourselves and the strength we possess, in order to gain what we wish. I hope we will not *have* to fight. No more Indians must be killed needlessly. White leaders will recognize our power and for once it will be *they* who must give in to *our* demands that they withdraw from our country and return eastward of the mountains. If possible, we will avoid war, but if it comes to war, we will not turn aside!"

There was great excitement among his listeners and as soon as the murmuring among them died away, Tecumseh went on. "From those tribes that I and you visit to convince, there will be some who will want to come with us immediately and join us in our nontribal village that we will establish. That is good and it should be done, for they will pass on to the tribes whence they sprang, words of our progress. They will help us so that when the time comes for the great sign to be given — a sign I will tell you of later, that will be given to all Indians at the same time — then those many thousands of warriors who are still in their villages will drop what they are doing and come at once to join their brother Indians who are at the great central village. In such a body we will face the whites, and they will fade away before us as the autumn leaves fade away before the winter wind.

"Now, what is most important is that while our preparation is going on, *we must not show it!* We must, at all costs, abide by our treaties with the whites. When whites infringe on these treaties, we must overlook it, though it angers us to do so. There will be occasions when we must temporarily swallow our pride, and this will be one of the greater difficulties to overcome. At such times, if necessary, we must fall back when the Shemanese nudge us. We must then turn our cheeks and pretend to be rabbits and under no pretext must we take up the hatchet against the whites until — and unless! — there is no other choice, and then not until I myself give the sign. We must profess a peaceable intent in all matters until we are ready. If there is any possibility of accomplishing our aims without warfare, then this must be the course we follow. But, war or not, it will be done. And the facts of what we are doing must be kept from the whites. No outsider must ever be allowed to sit in on the councils, and those who feel they have a right to sit in but are against us —

those such as Spemica Lawba and Winnemac and William Wells — must be denied.

"We ourselves, all of us, must faithfully, honestly and forever bury whatever past insults and hostilities and animosities have risen between us, and each of us, as individuals, must treat every other, regardless of his tribal background, as no less than a brother *Indian* fighting at his side for the same cause.

"Finally," he concluded, "when the period of waiting and building and growing is over, we will demand the return of our lands. With such a great unified force to give power to our demand, there is every reason to hope and believe the whites will leave our land peaceably. But if they will not, then I will give the signal. If and when this unmistakable sign is given, our irresistible wave of warriors will wash across the face of the land and drown every white man who has not the sense to flee east of the mountains to the east."

CHAPTER XVII

December 14, 1804

LTHOUGH Spemica Lawba had been inside the great estate called Grouseland many times, he never ceased inwardly to marvel at the elegance of it. No other structure in the Northwest Territory could begin to compare to the impressive and expansive governor's mansion in this wilderness settlement of Vincennes. The very finest of furnishings and embellishments filled the thirteen rooms — from finely made overstuffed sofas and chairs to huge mirrors, chandeliers and exquisite imported rugs over burnished hardwood floors. A great curving staircase in the entry parlor swept graciously to the second floor, its broad, polished balustrade superbly hand-carved. Four enormous marble-faced fireplaces terminated in a quartet of proud chimneys jutting fully nine feet higher than the tallest part of the mansard roof. A beautiful mahogany piano, polished to almost mirror finish, graced the drawing room for the use of the governor's lady, Anna, and a large staff of uniformed slaves kept the many items of silver and brass carefully free of any hint of tarnish and the carved mantels and doors and bannister uprights free of dust.

Surrounding this mansion of Governor William Henry Harrison were meticulously landscaped gardens and orchards, beyond which was dense woodland with a sizable population of

ruffed grouse, whence the estate's name had originated. Anticipating the many Indian councils that would be held on the
grounds in the future, the governor had had extensive arbors
built for the cooling shade they would provide, augmented by
grapevines planted at their corners. Numerous statues, large and
small, bestowed a regal air to the gardens. Harrison seemed to
take it all for granted. He seldom seemed overimpressed by anything and, though noted for a rare, explosive temper, the governor very rarely allowed his emotions to be witnessed in any
circumstance.

Today was one of the exceptions.

In the years he had spent serving William Henry Harrison in
one capacity or another, Spemica Lawba had never seen his em-
ployer so excited and pleased as now. At completing his first
reading of the express that had just arrived from the east, Harrison had let out a yell and leaped from his seat and even lost
his usual composure to the extent of doing a little jig. Now,
from his seat in the governor's office on the first floor of the
great Grouseland mansion, Spemica Lawba watched as Harrison read the message a second time, chortling to himself.

"Johnny," the governor said, looking up at him, "we did it!
This," he held up the message, "is from President Jefferson.
The Congress has ratified the St. Louis Treaty!"

Since Johnny Logan had had no part whatever in helping to
make that treaty, he was mystified by Governor Harrison's use
of the term "we," but he smiled nonetheless. He really did not
know much about the treaty except that it involved the cession
of an enormous tract of land to the United States by the Sac
and Fox tribes. Had he been more familiar with what had
brought the treaty about and what it involved, he might have
lost a great deal of faith in the governor's often repeated claim:
"I always have the very best interests of the Indians foremost in
my heart."

The treaty was one that Harrison had consummated less than
two months previously, acting on instructions from President

Thomas Jefferson and Secretary of War Henry Dearborn. Recurrent raids by the Sac Indians on settlers moving into the middle Mississippi River Valley and the western Illinois Country had convinced the United States that the only way to end the peril was to buy the land from them so they would have no excuse for future attacks of like nature.

Arriving in St. Louis, Harrison found that his advance agents had done exactly as he'd ordered them to, which was to locate some Sac and Fox chiefs who might be inveigled into signing a treaty ceding land to the United States. They had brought in five such chiefs and it had made no difference at all to the governor that only two of these chiefs had any small degree of authority among the Sacs as a tribe, and that the other three were insignificant village chiefs. Nor had it made any difference that none of the chiefs involved even resided in the land to be ceded and that, instead, their villages were some distance up the Missouri River.

Governor Harrison had quickly drawn up a treaty, assisted by two interpreters and one Indian agent, and had dangled a paltry payment before the greedy eyes of the chiefs. They immediately agreed to the terms of the treaty and put their marks to it. One of the chiefs was a bit reluctant to sign, but since he was one of the more important of the little group, he was bribed into signing by being offered the life of a relative who had been jailed for murder. The act of bribery seemed of little consequence to the treaty commissioners. The five chiefs signed and thus, in the eyes of the United States government, the entire populations of Sac and Fox Indians were thereby committed to abide by the terms of the treaty. And such terms they were!

In exchange for an annuity of $400 for the Foxes and $600 for the Sacs, plus gifts to the five Indian signers worth less than $2,235, the Americans received full cession to an area of fifty-one *million* acres! Mostly in the Illinois Country, the region ceded was bounded on the north by the Wisconsin River, on the east by the Fox River of the Illinois Country, on the southeast by the Illinois River and on the west by the Mississippi — plus a parcel approximately eighty miles by one hundred miles along the Missouri River west of the Mississippi.

Immediately, Harrison sent the signed treaty to the President, who submitted it to Congress without delay. The Congress had acted with amazing speed in ratifying the treaty, and it was word of the ratification that had today caused such elation in the normally staid William Henry Harrison. His uncharacteristic behavior quickly subsided. He laid the paper down on his desk and turned his attention to Spemica Lawba, clearing his throat as he did so.

The thirty-year-old Shawnee he called Johnny Logan was one of his most trusted and dependable agents, among a network of about thirty agents Harrison had by this time developed, including Indians, half-breeds and whites. Along with Spemica Lawba, William Wells and Winnemac, these agents included such men as Christopher Miller, who had been raised a captive of the Shawnees and was presently working in the general area of Fort Defiance; Thomas Forsyth, a trader — formerly British and now American — among the Potawatomies in the area of Peoria Lake in Illinois; Jack Lalime among the Potawatomies, he being the Fort Dearborn interpreter in the little settlement of Chicago at the southern end of Lake Michigan; Cornelius Washburn among the Kickapoos and Sacs on the Mississippi at the mouth of the Illinois River; and Shadrach Bond among others of the Kickapoos on the east side of the Mississippi south of St. Louis in the region of the old Indian villages of Cahokia and Kaskaskia.

Harrison cleared his throat a second time. "Well, Johnny," he said, "that's the sort of treaty it is so important for you to help me arrange with the Miamis and other tribes concerned in the region of Fort Wayne. Winnemac is already working on that, as you know, and Wells, too, but your assistance is always vital. Should we be able to get a measure similar to this," he tapped the document he had just received, "enacted in the region of the Wabash River, enormous benefit will be reaped by the Indians."

"I'll be doing all I can to help, Governor."

"Excellent! I knew I could count on you. Now, what's been happening among the Shawnees?"

Johnny Logan shrugged — a gesture he had long ago picked up in his association with the whites. "Nothing much. My chief, Catahecassa, still adheres to the Greenville Treaty in every respect, although he has been approached several times by emissaries from the British asking for his support in the event war should ever come again between the British and the Americans."

"As well it might," Harrison said, "considering the reports I've been getting of how they keep fomenting unrest toward us among the tribes. I don't know how much longer President Jefferson can tolerate these unfriendly measures on the part of the British." He cocked an eye at the Shawnee. "I presume Black Hoof rejected such advances?"

"Yes sir. He told them he was obliged by honor and for the good of his tribe to continue to abide by the terms of the Greenville Treaty."

"Fine, fine! He's a good man. Now, then, what's this I hear about a one-eyed Shawnee attempting to set himself up as medicine man and prophet among the Shawnees?"

"The man's name," Johnny said slowly, "is Lowawluwaysica. He is one of the small group who broke away from the tribe following the Greenville Treaty, but who returned some time ago. His leaning has always been somewhat toward medicine and the mystical and he has been learning many of the treatments and spells from the medicine men of various villages. He is harmless, and there is probably no likelihood of his ever becoming more prominent among the Shawnees, since our principal medicine man and prophet is old Penegashega, who is very healthy and quite jealous of his position in the tribe."

"All right, it seems there's nothing to be concerned about there. What about the split-away group? Are they still in that Delaware village on the White River?"

"Yes sir, they are. Buckangehela's village. They remain very quiet."

"I'm sure they'll stay that way, too," Harrison said briskly. "Now, what I'd like you to do is head back up to the upper Wabash and see if there's any way you can assist Wells and Winnemac in convincing the Miamis that it is in their best interest to cede to the government that area of land we've discussed." That area, Spemica Lawba knew, adjoined the six-miles-square area presently occupied by Vincennes and Grouseland, and extended quite some distance northward up the Wabash. "If you can get them to agree, be sure to bring me word of it immediately. Good luck."

It was a dismissal. Johnny Logan stood up, dipped his head in farewell to the governor, and strode from the mansion. Once again, as he had while he was speaking with the governor, he wondered if he should have told Harrison that his mother, uncles and stepfather were the leaders of that group of Shawnees that were residing in Chief Buckangehela's village on the White River . . . and that the would-be prophet, Lowawluwaysica, was his uncle.

CHAPTER XVIII

September 22, 1805

OU HAVE turned your back to us, Spemica Lawba. We are your blood, yet you have turned your back to us and chosen to serve him who is the enemy of all Indians."

The words of Tecumapese were spoken softly in response to her son's refusal to leave Wapatomica and come to live with them under Tecumseh's leadership, yet they were like hammer blows to Spemica Lawba and inwardly he winced as they struck him. He had hoped their reunion today after so long a separation would be a happy one, but it was not turning out that way.

"I have not forgotten where my blood is, Mother," he replied, his own words far more stiff than he meant them to be. "Your welfare and Wasegoboah's and that of my uncles is still very important to me."

"Then you have chosen a strange way of showing it," she replied. Her features were without expression but he thought he detected a faint quaver of emotion in her voice and it gave him hope that the rift between them could still be repaired.

They were in the Shawnee village of Tawa on the Auglaize River, little more than an hour's ride from Wapatomica, and he reached out impulsively and touched her arm. "Please," he said, "you are so near now to Wapatomica, won't you come with me after this meeting is over," he indicated the waiting crowd of Indians with a sweep of his arm, "and finally meet Pskipahcah Ouiskelotha and your grandsons?"

Tecumapese was tempted and it was only with the greatest of effort that she masked how she felt, hid from his view the yearning within her to embrace him and agree to go with him to see the wife of her son, whom she had never met, and the offspring of their union, her grandchildren, who were strangers to her. Nevertheless, she shook her head slowly and, as his hand dropped away, her words remained cold.

"Not so long as there is this distance between us. Ten summers ago you made your choice and turned your back to us who are your blood."

"You say I made my choice, Mother," he reminded, protesting, "but it was *I* who stayed with our people and it was *you* and Tecumseh and the others who left and never returned. That was your choice and I do not fault you for having made it, but should this be a wall that remains between us?"

"The wall," Tecumapese countered, "was erected by you, not by us. Our lodge was always open to you. You had only to open the gate in that wall and walk through to take your place beside us, but you chose instead to serve him who seeks only to take from the Indians what is rightfully theirs. Now the gate is locked and the wall goes too deep for you to dig beneath it, extends too far for you to go around, and is too high for you to climb. It will remain this way so long as you choose to wear the name Johnny Logan."

She turned away from him then and walked toward the wegiwa where Tecumseh and the rest of their party were staying temporarily, the tears she could no longer restrain streaking her cheeks, but not seen by her son. It was still some time until the assembly began — until what this crowd had gathered to hear was spoken — and so, instead of rejoining the others in the wegiwa, she walked to the river bank and stood quietly gazing at the water swirling past, her heart still heavy with thoughts of Spemica Lawba.

He is so like me, she thought, and like Tecumseh as well: proud and unbending once a decision is made he feels is correct. She breathed out a soft, sorrowful sound. Maybe one day, when the grand plan of Tecumseh became clear to all, he would then come back to them and they would be a family again. But not now, not yet. There were still too many obstacles remaining in the road. Perhaps one of the greatest of these could be overcome by the time this day had ended, as Tecumseh had said was possible, but she was unsure. It was not Tecumseh she doubted, it was Lowawluwaysica, with all his many faults to which Tecumseh seemed so blind. Deep in her heart she feared that one day Tecumseh's faith in their younger brother would be his undoing. Today, despite Lowawluwaysica's almost complete failure in his role as part of the great plan, Tecumseh was risking more than ever on him.

A surge of warmth and pride filled her as she recalled Tecumseh's return to the White River village following his long absence to distant tribes and his account of what he had accomplished on his journey. Word of his returning had long preceded him and his inner council were all on hand when he showed up: her husband, Wasegoboah, of course, as well as her younger brothers, Kumskaka and Lowawluwaysica. The Wyandot chief, Roundhead, was there as well, still resplendent in garb and ornamentation, and Chaubenee and Sauganash had come, bringing with them a Potawatomi chief named Skesh, whom Chaubenee had recruited. He was only one of a great many to whom Chaubenee and Sauganash had carried Tecumseh's doctrine in the lower Wisconsin and Michigan Country and throughout the entire Indiana Territory, which embraced the Illinois Country. The two had won many converts to the great plan; converts who merely awaited a summons.

The group had listened in fascination as Tecumseh told them not only of the great progress he had made, but equally of his failures in some areas. Already he had more tribes firmly aligned behind him than any other chief had ever gathered, yet he admitted they were not enough. Though he had traveled phenomenal distances, he told them he would have to travel even farther, work even harder, to bring the grand plan to completion. He admitted, as well, that the Americans had inadvertently helped convince many of the western tribes to join him. Those tribes had long felt themselves secure beyond the barrier created by the Missitheepi, but now the Americans had sent out two significant exploratory expeditions — one under an officer named Pike, to the very headwaters of the Missitheepi in the Minnesota country, and another under two captains, Lewis and Clark, which had gone up the Missouri and into the Rockies and headed toward the great western sea beyond. With such penetrations already in progress, many of the tribes realized that before long settlers would follow. For the first time, Indian nations in those lands were growing nervous.

It had been to his brothers that Tecumseh had left the responsibility of convincing the homeland tribes to accept his plan while he traveled to more distant places for the same purpose. Kumskaka, moving among the Kickapoo, Wea, Muncies and Delaware, had had moderate success, but Lowawluwaysica, among other Shawnees and Miamis, almost none. Before his departure, Tecumseh had given his one-eyed brother a great many predictions to relay to the Shawnees and other Indians here, as if those predictions were Lowawluwaysica's own. He had done so and they had all come to pass, as Tecumseh had known they would. This had brought the ugly one-eyed Shawnee some little recognition as a prophet, but it was only his own image that had improved, not Tecumseh's. He was singularly unsuccessful in lining up much support for Tecumseh, mainly because Lowawluwaysica was heartily disliked and his motives had always been suspect. He had even failed to sway such chiefs as Michikiniqua of the Miamis and Blue Jacket of his own Shawnees, both of whom were friends of Tecumseh. Michikiniqua felt the plan was dishonorable in view of the Greenville Treaty, while Blue Jacket was not fully convinced it was the proper thing to do. Many other Shawnee chiefs were suspicious, feeling that Tecumseh was merely trying a different method to usurp the authority of Catahecassa, aspiring to the post of principal chief to which, by Shawnee law and tradition, he was not qualified.

Tecumseh had no such intention and it bothered him that the belief was so prevalent among the Shawnees and that Lowawluwaysica had been so unsuccessful in attempts to convince their own people otherwise. How could they expect to get such home area tribes as the Miamis, Delawares, Ottawas, Potawatomies, and Wyandots to pledge their support to Tecumseh's proposed amalgamation if not even their brother Shawnees would do so? In an effort to rectify this, and with his principal followers behind him, Tecumseh had begun a tour to the villages of these homeland tribes. Increasingly, as they traveled, Tecumapese had become more distressed to see that many were so set in their ways, so blinded by their own importance and so fearful of losing their positions of leadership to Tecumseh, that they gave him and his followers short shrift.

Then, just as they arrived here in Tawa, with prospects dim, an abrupt turnabout occurred. An epidemic of severe stomach sickness struck and before sunset of that day, the venerable old Shawnee Prophet, Penegashega, had died. At once Tecumseh had called his followers into a private council in this wegiwa provided for their use and it was to Lowawluwaysica that he directed most of his comments.

"This is a bad sickness that has struck our Shawnee brothers," he said, "and it is not yet over. More than twenty have been afflicted and already Penegashega has died. What is yet to come provides us an opportunity we must not let pass. Lowawluwaysica, with the predictions I have given you in the past to speak, you have gained some recognition as a prophet. Now I want you to assemble all the warriors here, including those who are sick, and tell them you have had a vision in which you have seen that three more men will die of the sickness, but that at the end of five days the others who are afflicted will be well again, because you will cast the sickness from them. You will tell them that the three who are yet to die are men who are evil, men engaged in witchcraft, and they will die because you, Lowawluwaysica, will not save them for reason of what they are and what they do. You will also announce that at the end of five days, when you have cured all the others who are sick, you will speak publicly to them again, at which time you will tell them something of great importance. Do you understand?"

Lowawluwaysica nodded uncertainly and Tecumseh went over the instructions once again. It all came about precisely as Tecumseh predicted: three men died and the others recovered. Word of what was happening had spread, as Tecumseh had known it would, and now a much greater crowd had gathered, Spemica Lawba among them, to hear what Lowawluwaysica would say. There were more than just Shawnees here now; many of the Miamis had come, along with a number of Delawares, Wyandots, Ottawas, Chippewas and Potawatomies.

Now the time for that talk was almost at hand and Tecumapese turned away from the river and walked to the wegiwa where Tecumseh and his followers were in seclusion. Tecumseh rose to meet her as she entered.

"You spoke with him?" he asked.

She nodded, unsmiling. "He continues to be Johnny Logan, not our Spemica Lawba."

A small light of expectation in Tecumseh's eyes faded, and she knew he was not less disappointed than she, but he said no more on the subject. Turning back to the others he said, "It is time," and immediately they rose and followed him from the wegiwa to where the assemblage was gathered. They came close to where Spemica Lawba was sitting and though he smiled tentatively at them, they did not pause or recognize him. Tecumapese and Tecumseh, along with his lieutenants, moved to one side and seated themselves at the edge of the crowd, while Lowawluwaysica contined walking slowly to the front and stood there quietly while the general murmuring gradually died. Chaubenee, who disliked his leader's one-eyed brother and doubted his ability to carry it off, leaned toward their leader.

"Will he be able to do this, Tecumseh?" he whispered. "Can he make them believe?"

"Watch, my brother," Tecumseh replied just as softly. "Many in this village already believe, as do many others who have come from other towns. Those who do not yet believe will be caught up. During the night, while you and the others slept, I stayed up with Lowawluwaysica and instructed him. He now knows well what he is to say and how he is to say it. Listen!"

"Hear me, brothers!" Lowawluwaysica raised his hands and the final murmurings died. "You have witnessed my powers of prophecy in the past," Lowawluwaysica went on. "The things I said would be have come to pass. You have seen the three die as I predicted they would and you have witnessed the miracle I have performed in casting out the sickness that threatened your own lives."

Chaubenee, who had never heard him speak publicly, marveled at the strength in the voice of Tecumseh's younger brother as he continued.

"Hear me! You have known me until now by the name of Lowawluwaysica, but no longer! From this day forward I shall be known to all men as Tenskwatawa — One-with-Open-Mouth — and my mouth will be open with words to lead you to a better life, better health, a better future."

In the audience, Spemica Lawba's eyes had widened. Some strange thing had happened to his uncle. This was not the same man he had always known, who was weak and whining. An aura of power seemed to be flowing from the one now calling himself Tenskwatawa. The entire audience appeared to be sensing it as the speaker continued without pause.

"Penegashega the Prophet is dead. I say to you now that henceforth *I* am your Prophet and there is none other who is better qualified, none other who can do for you what I can do. Do I hear you say that you wish me to take this high office?" His words had picked up pace and even greater vibrancy as he spoke. He paused after this question and Roundhead smiled as the speaker cupped a hand behind each ear in an exaggerated posture of listening. There was a roar of approval and Chaubenee saw Tecumapese reach out and squeeze Tecumseh's wrist.

"*That* is our little brother?" she murmured.

Tecumseh wore a faint smile but made no response as the man who now called himself Tenskwatawa waited until the cries died away and then resumed speaking.

"I *am* Tenskwatawa," he said, "and my people call on me to serve them as Prophet. But such must be approved by the Shawnee Council. Since those wise men are among us today and since our Prophet is dead and there is little time to waste in lengthy discussion, I call on them now to say whether or not *I* am the Shawnee Prophet!"

Spemica Lawba was watching Tecumseh and saw him nod so imperceptibly that it was scarcely visible and he knew that this was exactly as his uncle had planned it, calculated to take the old Shawnee Council members in attendance by surprise and without opportunity to confer among themselves and gather opposition strength. It was a brilliant move, and Spemica Lawba admired him all the more for it. Other members of Tecumseh's group were obviously elated as Tenskwatawa pointed at the Shawnee Council members one by one, calling each by name and demanding a yes or no response. A few hesitated momentarily, obviously irked at having been maneuvered into this position but unwilling to risk the ire of the crowd with a negative reply. The vote was unanimous, and Tenskwatawa was officially the new Shawnee Prophet.

It was only the beginning. For three hours Spemica Lawba listened in amazement as Tenskwatawa delivered a spellbinding harangue. The one-eyed Shawnee decried the use by the previous Prophet, Penegashega, of bone bits, smooth stones, feath-

ers and other paraphernalia to make spells, which he declared
was a form of witchcraft and therefore evil. He orated against
the use of alcohol, which he admitted he had been guilty of
using in excess himself in the past, but would no more. He told
of having visions, of having been transported up into the clouds
and seeing the great Afterworld and learning what the Indians
must do to achieve the reward of going there. He warned darkly
of letting Indian women marry white men, saying it was the
white man's way of diluting the pure strain of Indian blood in
order to destroy the race and promising dire punishment to those
women who cohabited with white men. He emphasized the importance of all Indians everywhere in this land becoming one
people, united to common goals, just as those people who were
first of all Americans were of English, French, German, Irish,
Spanish, Scots and other origin. He told them the property of
one Indian must become the property of all, with each Indian
working for the common good of all Indians. He emphasized
that it was the duty of the young to cherish and support the
aged and infirm. He railed against the use of white man's clothing, saying that Indians were meant to wear the garb of their
ancestors — the skins of animals — and that they must return
to the old ways, which were wise and good. Since Moneto had
created the elk, deer, bear, bison and other creatures for their
use, he told them, it was evil to eat the flesh of hogs, cattle,
sheep and poultry, and likewise wrong to eat white man's wheat-
flour bread rather than the Indian's bread made of stone-ground
corn.

"You must believe," he said passionately, "that the Indian
race — not just this tribe or that, but the whole Indian race —
is superior to any other race on earth, for this is true! Now that
I am your Prophet, we have embarked on the trail that will
show our superiority to the world. Hear what I say! No Indian
who believes in the power and protectiveness of Moneto and has
confidence in himself ever needs to look to any man of another
race for help. We do not *need* help, as the whites would have us

believe. They have tried every means in their power to make us dependent upon them and upon those things they can provide for us, but the fathers of our fathers lived well without such things and so must we. We have allowed the white man to lead us away from our own beliefs and traditions. Now we must go back to them. We must return to a greater respect and admiration for Moneto and the many gifts and blessings he has bestowed upon us all."

His voice dropped abruptly and his listeners leaned forward intently so as not to miss a word. "The Great Spirit has revealed to me why it has been, in the past, that no matter whether we won battles or were defeated, in the end the Indian has always found himself on the side where lands and crops and lives have been lost, and the Great Spirit has shown me how all this can be changed.

"As I take on my duties as Prophet — as I begin a life of devotion to the cause and principles of the Indian people — this now I say to you: a tremendous power has been given to me by the Great Spirit to confound our enemies, cure all diseases, and prevent death by sickness or in battle. *I am your Prophet — Tenskwatawa!*"

Spemica Lawba was speechless with wonder at the transformation that had taken place in his one-eyed uncle, for whom he had never had any great love or respect. Before his eyes this unpleasant, ugly man had risen to new stature beyond any reasonable expectation — a transformation that had occurred even as he spoke. Tenskwatawa was, Spemica Lawba knew, still no more brave or truthful or above cruelty than he had been as Lowawluwaysica, nor had he lost his feral cunning or self-importance. Yet somehow, some way, his youngest uncle had this day been possessed of powers of persuasiveness and plausibility entirely equal to Tecumseh's. It was as if on this day and at this time and place, his youngest uncle had not only believed in what he was saying, he believed in *himself*, possibly for the first time in his life.

During the body of his speech, Tenskwatawa had referred to Tecumseh frequently and he had concluded his talk by telling his listeners that the village where Tecumseh was staying on the White River westward of Fort Greenville was no longer a Delaware village and certainly not a Shawnee village — that it was an *Indian* village and all who believed in him as Prophet and in Tecumseh as a leader who would guide them to greater glory than they had ever known before were welcome to come there and live. It was where, Tenskwatawa told them, he would himself be going to live beginning immediately. And from what could be determined by the crowd's reaction, it appeared that many would be joining him, and perhaps many more as word of this amazing day spread among the tribes.

Spemica Lawba admitted to himself that he was greatly impressed with today's performance and he knew others were, also. But as much as Tenskwatawa had been an amazingly inspired speaker this day, demanding almost hypnotic attention from his audience, Spemica Lawba had spent as much time surreptitiously watching Tecumseh as he had the speaker. He was, therefore, one of the very few on hand who had seen Tecumseh's noddings as various points were made. And it had come to him with great clarity that Tenskwatawa, however good his performance, had only been parroting what Tecumseh had instructed him to say. It was a conviction he was determined to keep to himself . . . at least for now.

Spemica Lawba had hoped to talk privately with Tecumseh after the speech, but he lost track of his uncle in the crowd and the next time he spied him, Tecumseh was leading his followers away on horseback. For the first time in a very long while, then, the old doubts assailed Spemica Lawba and he wondered if he had been wrong not to side with him.

CHAPTER XIX

April 2, 1806

HE PROPHET be damned!"

A stunned silence fell over the delegation of Delaware chiefs visiting William Henry Harrison at Vincennes, and immediately the governor regretted his outburst. But then he silently cursed the man again. The Prophet! That was all he heard about these days and he was sick of it. Somehow, all of his problems of late seemed to originate from the strange one-eyed Shawnee who'd come out of nowhere and proclaimed himself a prophet. What galled him most was that the stupid savages were so willing to accept him as such, as if he wasn't having difficulty enough dealing with them about real problems without having to get involved in their idiotic superstitions. He calmed himself and spoke in a level tone to the delegation's spokesman, Chief Peke-tele-mund.

"The man you call The Prophet, who presently lives in your village on the White River, has no more prophetic ability than I."

He waited patiently as Johnny Logan interpreted for him and, as the Shawnee finished, went on, with Johnny interpreting very nearly as swiftly as he spoke "You have been misled. Your people should all be told of this. You say he tells you that those who deal in magic and witchcraft should be burned at the stake?

By what right does he pretend to be God among you? By what foolishness do you and your chief, Buckangehela, accept what he says without proof? Are you such children as that?"

Harrison paused, waiting until Johnny's rapid-fire interpretation caught up. When the Indians politely waited for the governor to go on, he shook his head and pointed toward the other end of the canvas-covered arbor. "Over on those tables," he told them in a gentler voice, "you will find food and drink. Refresh yourselves while I write a letter for you to take back to your people, that they may know the truth."

The governor strode off toward his Grouseland mansion as Johnny interpreted his final remarks. And when Peke-tele-mund and his delegation moved to the table and began to eat the bread, cold boiled chicken and slices of beef that had been prepared for them, Spemica Lawba was still watching as the governor entered the great house. He knew Harrison lately had grown exasperated over Tenskwatawa's growing influence and considered The Prophet to be a pawn of the British operating out of their Fort Malden at Amherstburg, across the river and downstream from Detroit.

That Harrison had no inkling yet of the existence of Tecumseh was not surprising. Few whites had ever heard of him and even those few had no conception of how powerful he was becoming among the tribes. By the same token, however, there were few Indians apart from Spemica Lawba and Tecumseh's inner council who realized that virtually all the things Tenskwatawa did or said — including the predictions he continued to make — were at the direction of his older brother. Yet, Spemica Lawba had no intention of enlightening the governor about Tecumseh, irrespective of how much his own basic philosophy differed from his uncle's. However long it took Harrison to realize just who was the power behind Tenskwatawa was soon enough.

Spemica Lawba had to admit that there was a certain amount of justification in Harrison's conviction that the British were behind many of the troubles he was having, but it had little to do with Tenskwatawa. The governor had consistently received reports from his spies, including Spemica Lawba, of British agitation against the Americans. The British tendrils — most often in the guise of traders or Indian agents such as Simon Girty, Matthew Elliott, William Caldwell, Thomas McKee and others — stretched deep into the territory the Americans considered theirs, and wherever the Americans could be undermined among the Indians, it was done. Here a trader decried desecration of Indian burial grounds by the Americans; there a trader stirred resentment over Zebulon Pike's expedition up the Mississippi; elsewhere a trader warned of the ramifications of the Lewis and Clark expedition to the far west. Throughout the tribes they depicted William Henry Harrison as a ravenous monster gobbling up the lands, and as further proof of the American land hunger, they pointed to the fact that Ohio had now become a state and Michigan had received status as a territory in its own right and with its own governor at Detroit, William Hull.

Spemica Lawba was uneasy, as were many others who could detect the signs. There was the smell of war in the air, still far off but growing stronger with each passing month as relations between Americans and British deteriorated, the old wounds of the Revolutionary War still festering. Harrison was aware of it, too, and had helped inculcate President Jefferson with it. And, though Jefferson had taken some steps to smooth the ruffled waters between the Indians and the Americans, thus far his efforts had borne little fruit. The matter of the trade goods was a case in point. The President ordered Harrison to endeavor to divert this seeming attachment developing in the Indians for the British by offering the Indians better prices for their furs than the British could pay and by selling them trade goods at prices much cheaper than the British could match. However, as soon as the British learned of it, they had turned the tables and hired Indians to buy goods for them from the Americans at prices cheaper than they normally could be brought over from England.

Harrison was attributing much of the Indian unrest to The
Prophet and this was the reason he had grown so agitated earlier
at the constant reference to Tenskwatawa by the Delaware delegation. While Chief Buckangehela liked Tecumseh and had enjoyed having him and his followers stay at the White River village, the Delaware leader had lately been growing nervous. On
the one hand he feared The Prophet's seeming mystical powers;
on the other he feared that having Tenskwatawa residing in his
village might damage the cordial relationship he had long shared
with the governor. Besides, The Prophet was now beginning to
suggest that any who did not believe him was running a great
risk of having his own people rise up and burn them alive at the
stake. That was why Buckangehela had finally sent the delegation to Harrison — to disavow any anti-American feeling among
his Delawares and to state that he was not responsible for what
The Prophet said and did that might adversely affect the
Americans.

Spemica Lawba broke off from his musings to see that the
governor was returning and he moved to meet him. Harrison
handed him an envelope that was closed with a glob of wax on
which was a deep impression of the governor's official seal. The
letter was addressed to Chief Buckangehela of the Delawares.

"Go back with them to their village, Johnny," he ordered.
"Hand this personally to Buckangehela. After he reads it, en-
courage him to show it to every other chief he can."

"Yes sir."

The Shawnee turned back toward the delegation, wondering
what was in the letter and content that he would soon know,
since Buckangehela could not read English and Spemica Lawba
would have to translate it for him.

CHAPTER XX

April 28, 1806

HE STOCKY, barrel-chested Buckangehela, his people
clustered about him, broke the seal of the letter from
Governor Harrison and then stared without compre-
hension at the penned words on the sheets. After a moment he
shrugged and handed the missive back to Spemica Lawba.

"Read," he said.

Spemica Lawba read aloud, smoothly and quite flawlessly
converting the written English to the spoken Delaware dialect:

> *"My Children:*
>
> *My heart is filled with grief, and my eyes are dissolved in
> tears at the news which has reached me. You have been cele-
> brated for your wisdom above all the tribes of red people who
> inhabit this great island. Your fame as warriors has extended
> to the remotest nations, and the wisdom of your chiefs has gained
> you the appellation of grandfathers from all the neighboring
> tribes . . ."*

There was a gasp from the Delawares and both Buckangehela
and Peke-tele-mund frowned. Spemica Lawba himself was
stunned that Harrison had made such an error. By no stretch of
the imagination had the Delawares, formerly vassals of the Iro-

quois, gained recognition as warriors. Further, only one tribe, the Wyandots, offshoot of the Hurons, was referred to by other tribes with the term "grandfather," a title of enormous respect. For Harrison to have written these words was tantamount to his ridiculing the Delawares and insulting the Wyandots, and the governor had lost considerable face for his blunder. Spemica Lawba recovered his poise in a moment and read on:

". . . *From what cause, then, does it proceed that you have departed from the wise counsels of your fathers and covered yourselves with guilt? My Children, tread back the steps that you have taken, and endeavor to regain the straight road which you have abandoned. The dark, crooked, and thorny one which you are now pursuing will certainly lead you to endless woe and misery. But who is this pretended prophet who dares to speak in the name of the great Creator? Examine him. Is he more wise and virtuous than you are yourselves, that he should be selected to convey to you the orders of your God? Demand from him some proofs at least of his being the messenger of the Deity. If God had really empowered him, He has doubtless authorized him to perform miracles that he may be known and received as a prophet. If he is really a prophet, ask of him to cause the sun to stand still or the moon to alter its course, the rivers to cease to flow, or the dead to rise from their graves. If he does these things, you may believe he has been sent from God. He tells you that the Great Spirit commands you to punish with death those who deal in magic, and that he is authorized to point them out. Wretched delusion! Is then the Master of Life obliged to appoint mortal man to punish those who offend Him? Has He not the thunder and the power of nature at His command? And could He not sweep away from the earth a whole nation with one sweep of His arm? My Children, do not believe that the great and good Creator of Mankind has directed you to destroy your own flesh; and do not doubt that if you pursue this abominable wickedness His vengeance will overtake and crush you.*

The above is addressed to you in the name of the Seventeen

Fires. I now speak to you from myself, as a friend who wishes nothing more sincerely than to see you prosperous and happy. Clear your eyes, I beseech you, from the mist which surrounds them. No longer be imposed on by the arts of an imposter. Drive him from your town, and let peace and harmony prevail amongst you. Let your poor old men and women sleep in quietness, and banish from their minds the dreadful idea of being burnt alive by their friends and countrymen. I charge you to stop your bloody career; and if you value the friendship of your great father, the President; if you wish to preserve the good opinion of the Seventeen Fires, let me hear by the return of the bearer that you have determined to follow my advice.

> *Your friend and adviser,*
> *William Henry Harrison*
> *Governor — Indiana Territory"*

There was a long moment of silence as Spemica Lawba finished reading the letter, refolded it and slipped it back into its envelope. Chief Buckangehela was frowning as he considered the governor's challenge. He looked at Spemica Lawba as the messenger handed him the envelope.

"Your white chief wishes The Prophet to give us proof," he said. He nodded slowly. "Come with me, then, and we will lay this before him."

The chief turned and began walking toward the western edge of the village, Peke-tele-mund beside him, Spemica Lawba directly behind them and virtually the whole populace of the village following at a respectful distance. As they approached an extra-large wegiwa on a high bank above the river, two men emerged and stood awaiting them. When Buckangehela and Peke-tele-mund stopped, a dozen feet from the two Shawnees in the doorway, Spemica Lawba halted also. Tenskwatawa, a black eyepatch covering the empty socket, was scowling. Buckangehela opened his mouth to speak, but Tecumseh stopped him with an upraised hand and spoke first.

"Who is it I only partly see behind my Delaware friends?"

Spemica Lawba stepped forward. With only six years' difference in his age and Tecumseh's, the two looked much more like brothers than uncle and nephew. Even his voice, as he spoke, had a quality similar to Tecumseh's.

"I greet my uncles with respect and friendship. I came here to deliver to Chief Buckangehela — and to translate for him — a letter from Governor Harrison. I had looked forward to seeing you." He glanced beyond the brothers a moment, then met Tecumseh's gaze again. "I had also hoped to see my mother, whom I have not seen for too long."

"Tecumapese is on a journey," Tecumseh replied evenly. "My eyes are glad to see you; my heart is not, since it knows you come here as the agent of one whose aim is to harm the Indians."

Spemica Lawba answered him softly but firmly. "Indians and whites can live in peace, Tecumseh."

"You are incorrect, nephew," Tecumseh replied. "Indians and whites can *never* live in peace. They can only live close to one another *if* the Indian does what the white man wishes and moves aside when the white man stretches. All our history and that of other tribes has shown this to be true." His gaze shifted to the Delaware chief. "What has the white beaver written to you?"

Buckangehela stepped forward and handed him the letter, which Tecumseh accepted without looking at it. "He wishes us to demand proof," Buckangehela said, stepping back beside Peketele-mund and Spemica Lawba, "that Tenskwatawa is indeed The Prophet. Spemica Lawba will read it to you."

A peculiar expression came into Tenskwatawa's face and he glanced somewhat nervously at his older brother, who shook his head faintly. "I will read it myself," he replied.

Swiftly and flawlessly he read the letter aloud, smoothly translating the written English words into the Shawnee tongue. His one-eyed brother's expression became strained as he heard Harrison's words, but Tecumseh seemed unconcerned. He glanced at Tenskwatawa as he finished, an unspoken message passing between them, and immediately The Prophet let his gaze flash across his nephew and Peke-tele-mund and stop on Buck-angehela, whom he addressed.

"Let the messengers rest and eat. I will retire to my place and meditate on this to see what direction, if any, I shall receive from the Great Spirit in this matter."

Tenskwatawa turned and reentered the wegiwa and Tecumseh followed him. Taken by surprise, Buckangehela stood there a moment before turning on his heel and striding back toward the center of the village, the messenger, subchief and villagers following. Spemica Lawba was provided with food and drink and had hardly finished when he was summoned to return to the open area before the wegiwa of his uncles, where everyone was gathering. In a short while all four hundred Delaware residents of the village, plus half that many visitors, had assembled. Tecumseh stood quietly near the door of the wegiwa but Tenskwatawa had mounted a small knoll nearby and held both arms high until silence reigned. Then, with frequent interjections of "I am your Prophet!" Tenskwatawa launched into a harsh denunciation of the whites in general and William Henry Harrison specifically.

"It is very clear," he went on bitterly, "that the white chief Harrison does not know what he is talking about or he would never have referred to the Delawares as 'Grandfathers.' As for me," Tenskwatawa spat disgustingly to one side, "I have nothing but scorn for any Indian who believes what the white men says or writes. Since receiving the letter from Harrison, I have conferred with the Great Spirit, who is angry and has directed that you be given a sign.

"The white beaver, Harrison," he continued, "said that you should ask me, if I am really The Prophet — and I *am* your Prophet! — to cause the sun to stand still and that if I can do this, then you can believe that I have been sent from God. Those are his words, not mine! Therefore, listen now to what I have to say: Fifty days from this day there will be no cloud in the sky. Yet, when the sun has reached its highest point, at that moment will the Great Spirit take its blazing fire into his hand and hide it from us. The darkness of night will thereupon cover us and the stars will shine round about us. The birds will go to roost and the night creatures will awaken and stir. Then you will know, as the white chief, Harrison, has said, that your Prophet has been sent to you from Moneto. Go now, and wait. I have nothing more to say."

The Prophet turned and strode into the wegiwa, but as he passed Tecumseh a meaningful glance passed between them that was observed by Spemica Lawba. In that moment the latter knew beyond any doubt that the prophecy, though delivered by Tenskwatawa, had come from Tecumseh. For just an instant before Tecumseh followed Tenskwatawa into the wegiwa, his eyes met those of his nephew and, in that moment as well, Spemica Lawba knew that Tecumseh had read him clearly.

CHAPTER XXI

June 17, 1806

ORD OF Harrison's challenge and The Prophet's acceptance of it spread quickly throughout the tribes of the Northwest Territory, and so today a peculiar ritual was being enacted in villages all over. In mid-morning on this bright, beautiful day, the men, women and children left their abodes and assembled in the open, filled with expectancy. This was the day when the Shawnee who called himself Tenskwatawa would be proven to be a Prophet or a charlatan.

This was the fiftieth day . . . and at precisely noon there occurred a total eclipse of the sun.

In forests and fields the night-roving animals roused and began moving about, while confused birds of the day settled down to roost.

In the Indian villages there was consternation and fear and monumental awe for a Prophet so great he could command even the sun.

In Wapatomica, Spemica Lawba stood outside with his family. His arm moved around Pskipahcah Ouiskelotha's waist and he held her close. "I knew when I saw Tecumseh's eyes that it would come to pass," he murmured. "It is very bad. It will undo almost all I have worked for to keep peace between Indians and whites."

In Fort Wayne, William Wells stepped outside the door of his house, looked up and groaned at the spectacle, muttering, "There'll be hell to pay now."

In Chaubenee's village on Indian Creek, sixty-five miles west of Fort Dearborn at Chicago, he and his guest stared at the sky. Sauganash muttered "Tecumseh," and Chaubenee nodded, for they both knew.

In Roundhead's village on the south shore of Lake Erie, he and the Wyandot principal chief, Tarhe — The Crane —watched the eclipse open-mouthed. Roundhead said softly, "You see, it is as he said it would be." And Tarhe, custodian of the Greenville Treaty for all the tribes, upholder of all its articles and staunch advocate for peace, was wracked by a trembling that he could not control.

In Vincennes, William Henry Harrison cursed aloud at having been bested and wondered from whom Tenskwatawa had learned that a solar eclipse was to occur.

In the center of Buckangehela's village, Tenskwatawa lifted his arms and nearly seven hundred assembled Indians heard him cry, "Behold! Did I not prophesy truly? Darkness has shrouded the earth!"

And in his wegiwa in that White River village, Tecumseh sat quietly in the darkness.

CHAPTER XXII

July 13, 1809

EVEN THOUGH Governor Harrison continued to assure Spemica Lawba that the Greenville Treaty would continue to be honored by both sides and there would not be another war, the Shawnee was sure in his own mind that war would ultimately come.

Tecumseh's influence among the tribes — even those at great distances — had increased phenomenally over these past three years. He was rarely seen in the Northwestern Territory anymore, being constantly on the move and winning ever more converts to his grand plan. News had filtered to Spemica Lawba that virtually all tribes eastward of the Rocky Mountains, from Canada to the Gulf of Mexico, had been visited by the visionary Shawnee. Wherever he spoke, large crowds assembled to hear him. Unlike Indian orators of the past, Tecumseh did not shout or coax, wheedle or beseech; neither did he threaten or demand or coerce; he merely spoke calmly in a strong voice that carried to every ear, giving them his vision — his dream of one people, *Indians*, united in a powerful amalgamation against which no outside force could stand. They were inspired by the concept, for he gave them a dream that was more than a dream. He offered them power — more power than they had ever known as individuals, as villages, as tribes or as confederacies. It was a solid plan that held every likelihood of restoring to them all their lands, their pride, their self-respect.

He gave them hope.

With Spemica Lawba acting as interpreter, Governor Harrison had met with Tenskwatawa twice at Grouseland. Each meeting had been followed by long private conversations with Spemica Lawba. Though his trusted Shawnee aide never fully revealed all he had learned or even that Tecumseh and Tenskwatawa were his uncles, Harrison began putting pieces together for himself. From those meetings and others with William Wells, Thomas Forsyth, Winnemac, Jack Lalime, Shadrach Bond and others of his spies, he formed a picture that was not merely disconcerting — it was frightening.

Harrison knew now that Tecumseh and Tenskwatawa were brothers and that they had, because of the nervousness of their Delaware hosts, moved away from Buckangehela's village and established a new nontribal village on a tributary of the Wabash River. It was on the site where an ancient village had once stood named Kithtippecanoe, and this new village was named after both that village and the stream on which it was situated — Tippecanoe. Harrison also knew that The Prophet was acting chief there during Tecumseh's prolonged absences and that for this reason many people were calling the village Prophet's Town. But the governor was now convinced that while Tenskwatawa had a certain amount of power and was held in awe by many Indians, it was his elder brother, Tecumseh, who was the mind and power behind him. Word had trickled to Harrison of the travels of Tecumseh and there were hints of some great plan he was advocating that would give the Indians such power that the whites would not be able to stand against him. He had heard, as well, that the accurate predictions so often made by The Prophet were actually prophecies envisioned by Tecumseh and merely relayed to the Indians by the one-eyed Tenskwatawa.

The most disturbing aspect of what he heard was that Tecumseh was predicting some kind of sign that would be evident to all the tribes at the same time, and when that sign occurred, Tecumseh's great plan — whatever it was — would be activated. Once activated, the consequences would be the worst thing that ever happened to the whites in America. The governor could not conceive of what sort of signal could simultaneously be received by all tribes and he tended to scoff at it, yet he was worried. He felt sure Spemica Lawba knew the details of it, but his Shawnee aide continued to claim ignorance.

In point of fact, Spemica Lawba *had* heard more that he admitted to, but because what he knew was only hearsay, he withheld the information, fearful that if he told Harrison and the stories proved false, a great deal of trouble would be caused for no good purpose and further hamper his hope of peace. But while he did not tell Harrison of it, he discussed the matter at length with Pskipahcah Ouiskelotha as they walked aimlessly together through knee-high prairie grasses near Wapatomica.

"I have heard," he told his wife, "that Tecumseh has given to each of the principal chiefs a bundle of red sticks of the same size."

"But for what?" she asked, wrinkling her brow. "I don't understand."

"Nor do I, completely," he replied, with his characteristic shrug, "but I am given to believe that at each full moon every chief is to discard one stick from the bundle."

"Until they're all gone? But why?"

"No, until only one remains. When that time comes, they are to keep close watch of the night sky and before another moon comes, a sign will appear in the darkness above. The sign under which Tecumseh was born — the sign of The-Panther-Passing-Across; a great shooting star that will be pale green in color. Now this is supposedly not the great sign he has been predicting for so many years, but rather a preliminary one. As soon as it occurs, the remaining red stick held by each principal chief is to be cut into thirty equal pieces. One such piece is to be burned each day in the light of dawn."

"Until just one is left again?" Pskipahcah Ouiskelotha asked.
He nodded. "So I have heard. Then that last piece is to be
burned in the deepest dark of the following night. After that the
great sign is supposed to come."
     She stopped walking and faced him. "Well, what is it? Do you
know?" She appeared concerned.
     He shrugged again. "I'm not sure. I've heard whispers — bits
and pieces — but they don't make much sense. Some say the
inside of the earth will growl like an angry bear. Some say lakes
that have always existed will suddenly disappear and other lakes
will appear where they never were before. Some say the ground
will tremble with fear. Some say villages will collapse and all
the earthen jugs will be broken. There are even some who say
that *all* these things will happen at the same time, everywhere."
     "And when . . . *if* they do?" She linked her arm with his and
they began walking again. It was a little while before he answered.
     "Then all the warriors are to drop whatever they are doing,
take up their weapons and go at once to Tecumseh's new village,
Tippecanoe."
     "Well, what's supposed to happen when they get there?"
     "I don't know," Spemica Lawba said slowly. He shrugged
again. "I just don't know."
     A shiver ran through his wife and she pressed closer against
him. "I wish you didn't have to leave for Vincennes tomorrow
morning," she said.
     He nodded, agreeing, then added, "But I do."

At this same moment, far to the east in the United States
capital, the new Secretary of War, William Eustis, was writing
to Governor Harrison. The letter ordered Harrison, in the name
of President James Madison, to call a major council of the Indians at Fort Wayne this coming fall for the purpose of obtaining
another major land cession for the United States, since the land
obtained by the Greenville Treaty was now nearly all settled.

The acquisition Eustis had in mind was three million acres of rich Indiana Territory land, beginning at a point twenty-one miles north of Vincennes and extending northward and eastward. The northern edge of this proposed acquisition was hardly more than a few miles from a relatively new Indian village near the mouth of a stream emptying into the Wabash River.

Tippecanoe.

CHAPTER XXIII

September 30, 1809

I T WAS because the possibility of another war with England was looming and British agents were reported infiltrating into United States territory that William Henry Harrison chose three Shawnees as his bodyguard on the overland trip from Vincennes to Fort Wayne.

Relations with England had degenerated severely of late, and the smell of war was in the air. The British were boarding American ships in American territorial waters and impressing American crewmen to man British ships. Further, the British had placed an embargo on France and were preventing foreign shipping from entering French ports. They brazenly warned the United States in a document called "Orders in Council" that if any American ship headed for France, it would be seized on the open sea in nonterritorial waters.

Harrison's corps of spies reported from all quarters that British agents, moving about among the neutral Indians or those unfriendly to the Americans, were stepping up their activities in fomenting unrest. Only a short while ago the new governor-in-chief of Canada, Sir James Craig, gave explicit instructions along these lines to the British Indian Agent Matthew Elliott at Amherstburg. Sir James sent Elliott as an emissary to the various chiefs to sound out their loyalties in private and to ". . . impress upon them with delicacy and caution that England expects their aid in the event of war. Be certain to remind them that the Americans are out to steal their lands."

Therefore, with rumors floating about that British agents or unfriendly Indians might attempt to kill or kidnap Governor Harrison, a bodyguard of three topnotch guides was deemed essential. Foremost of these, of course, was Harrison's faithful spy of many years — Johnny Logan. The other two Shawnees were close friends of his own age, both also of Wapatomica. One was a large, good-natured man with an unusually expressive face that almost perpetually wore a smile. His name was Gituta — Otter — but the whites called him Captain John. The other, practically the opposite in size but almost equally good-natured, was Teopah Kouleelawba — Bright Horn — who was a very agile individual. Both were part of the small spy company that Spemica Lawba had formed at Governor Harrison's request over a year ago. Neither could speak or understand English, but both were quite as fluent as Spemica Lawba in the Miami dialect.

This latter talent, as things turned out, had scarcely been used. Having escorted Harrison from Vincennes, the four had arrived here fifteen days ago without incident and, from that point on, the three Shawnees were largely excluded from the negotiations. Most of those negotiations had been handled thus far by two other Harrison deputies, William Wells, and Winnemac, the Potawatomi village chief. Wells and Winnemac met their party and, though Wells seemed to be concerned over possible ramifications of the proposed land cession, Winnemac smiled crookedly and chortled over how he had "softened" the chiefs who had been opposed to the deal.

The three Shawnee companions were kept largely in the dark by Harrison in respect to what had already taken place here and what was still transpiring. Reasonably enough, they considered it merely another land cession being consummated as the result of rather extensive and fair bargaining with the Indians involved.

Matters may have taken a much different direction had the three known the truth.

William Wells knew that Tecumseh had nothing but scorn for him and the concern the former Miami was exhibiting now was a manifestation of his fear that when Tecumseh learned what had taken place — how he and Winnemac were threatening the Miamis into signing — he might cause problems, perhaps even an uprising among the Indians that would bloom into a new Indian war. It was then Wells seriously proposed to Harrison that Tecumseh be assassinated. However unscrupulous Harrison might have been in his greed for Indian land, he was not a murderer and he quickly put the quietus to the suggestion. But, as Sir James Craig was telling the Indians through Matthew Elliott, William Henry Harrison was not above cheating the Indians.

The land in question was owned mainly by the Miamis, though a small portion of it was Potawatomi. In the negotiations that took place, no influential chief of either tribe had been invited or was even aware that such negotiations were occurring. Winnemac, not only as Harrison's employee but as merely a minor village chief of the Potawatomies, had no authority whatever to sell even the Potawatomi land, much less that belonging to the Miamis.

At first the Miamis were not at all willing to sell and balked. At Harrison's order, a certain amount of whiskey was provided for "refreshment" and then the talks resumed. This pattern repeated itself time and again as the days passed. Gradually more pressure was placed on the Miamis, with Winnemac moving among the minor chiefs, coaxing, coercing, imploring and finally even threatening to make war on them. Harrison continued talking, painting the British in the worst possible colors, blaming them entirely for the fact that the Miamis were now in a position where selling their land was the only remaining option. Finally, today, Harrison deliberately sent Johnny Logan, Bright Horn and Captain John on a wholly inconsequential errand that would keep them away most of the day. The governor did so because lately Johnny Logan had begun to question some of Harrison's actions. The white leader wanted to avoid adding any fuel to whatever suspicions Johnny Logan may have begun to harbor about his motives. And while the trio of Indian spies was gone, Harrison addressed the assembled Indians, his voice ringing with sincerity and a touch of reproach.

"This is the first request your new Father, President Madison, has ever made of you. It will be the last — he wants no more of your land. Agree to the proposition which I now make you and send on some of your wise men to take him by the hand. He will set your heart at ease. He will tell you that he will never make another proposition to you to sell your lands."

And so, with the pressure from Wells and Winnemac — for which they were well paid — and Harrison's promise of abundant whiskey after the treaty was signed, the attending Indians gave in. The documents were duly signed, followed by a drunken revel during which one of the Miami warriors was killed.

With the Fort Wayne Treaty signed, Harrison was jubilant. He had done it again! The United States now owned another forty-seven hundred square miles — an area of some three million acres. In direct obedience to the directive he'd received from President Madison to that effect, Harrison had paid next to nothing for it . . . less than seven dollars per square mile. He was well aware that in the not too distant future, American settlers would be paying the government two dollars per *acre* for this same land — a profit potential of six million dollars.

Harrison retired to his tent and began writing his report to Secretary of War Eustis, saying, in part:

> . . . *The compensation given for this cession of lands is as low as it could possibly be made. I think, upon the whole, that the bargain is a better one for the United States than any that has been made by me for lands south of the Wabash. . . . As soon as the treaty has been ratified and a sales office has been opened, there will be several hundred families along this Tract. . . . If any ill blood yet remains, a little attention to the influential chiefs will soon remove it. . . .*

CHAPTER XXIV

July 3, 1810

M UCH AS Spemica Lawba felt that Tecumseh's efforts were futile and would ultimately fail, his admiration for his uncle was very strong. The more cause his uncle had for anger, it seemed, the less he submitted to it. It seemed only to make him think more clearly and become more convincing to those who heard him.

There were still times when Spemica Lawba wavered in his own beliefs and thought that perhaps Tecumseh was correct, that there could never be peace with equality between Indians and whites. But the feeling didn't last; he had associated with the whites too long and was too aware of their resources, not only their unending sources of manpower and supplies, but also the benefits inherent in their culture for the red man. There were times as well — such as in the outraged aftermath of Harrison's latest treaty — when he suspected the governor of perfidy; of using him only to further the cause of the whites and diminish that of the Indians. He'd had these feelings before and each time Harrison had glibly explained away the fears and suspicions. In this latest matter, it had taken the governor hours of rhetoric and entreaty to reestablish in Johnny Logan's mind the sincere belief that the treaty would, in the long run, prove to be of as much benefit to the Indians as to the whites.

Perhaps Johnny would not have been convinced of Harrison's sincerity even then, had he not been in the position of assessing Catahecassa's position in present matters involving Tecumseh. Catahecassa's stance in opposing Tecumseh was evidently based more on jealousy of Tecumseh's great influence among the tribes and fear that somehow Tecumseh would usurp his power than on a clear vision of the future for his people. In other words, Spemica Lawba admitted to himself, his opinion was that Catahecassa was going in the right direction but for the wrong reasons.

Catahecassa, now eighty-four and still highly venerated in the tribe, sat today in council with Tecumseh, along with a score of minor chiefs of his tribe and several hundred Shawnee warriors who still adhered to the dictates of their principal chief. Spemica Lawba was part of that council taking place in Catahecassa's Town on the Auglaize and he, as did most of those in attendance, had thought Tecumseh would make no further efforts to convince the Shawnees to embrace his plan. This was especially true in view of the fact that at their last meeting, Catahecassa had made it clear he would, to his final breath if need be, prevent his Shawnees from following Tecumseh on a path that must lead to war with the Americans.

"We have fought enough," he had said then. "Always we have been first to suffer the bites of the white dogs. No more. We will not join the whites in their struggle against one another, and we will not join you in your struggle against them."

"And I will not," Spemica Lawba murmured under his breath, finishing Catahecassa's statement for him in a more straightforward manner, "turn over my leadership of the Shawnees to you or anyone else." That he had even had such a thought, though not overheard in his comment, caused another surge of guilt to rise in him.

What had changed Tecumseh's mind about making one final effort to convince Catahecassa was that Tecumseh's old friend, Blue Jacket, had become so disenchanted with Catahecassa's unrealistically bullheaded stand and with what was happening to Indian lands that he had begun leaning strongly toward Tecumseh. When word had spread of Harrison's latest maneuver, with the help of Winnemac and Wells, in getting a cession of three million more acres of Indian lands, he was beside himself with anger and had sent word to Tecumseh to come to Catahecassa's Town to address the neutral chiefs and warriors. When he did so, Blue Jacket's message had said, at that time Blue Jacket would himself side with Tecumseh in direct and open opposition to Catahecassa. Together they stood a good chance of swinging the scales in their own favor.

So Tecumseh had arrived with his entourage, only to be devastated by the news that Weh-yeh-pih-ehr-sehn-wah — he who was known as Blue Jacket — had died a few days previously of a fever. And Catahecassa, though unable to prevent the council that had convened, refused to meet in preliminary council with Tecumseh.

Now, standing before the assembled Shawnee, Delaware, Miami and Potawatomi chiefs and warriors, Tecumseh held up a sheet of paper for all to see. "This," he told them, "is a letter from the white devil, Harrison, shown to me with pride by Chief Catahecassa. It praises Catahecassa for his peaceful disposition." In a wholly unexpected movement, he suddenly crumpled the paper and threw it into the small council fire burning between himself and the audience. It burst into flames and was consumed, and when Tecumseh spoke again there was sorrow and bitterness in his voice.

"So much for praise from our greatest enemy!" His gaze stopped momentarily on Spemica Lawba. "If your Governor Harrison were here, I would serve him in the same way." He looked away from his nephew and across the assemblage again for a long silent time. When finally he spoke once more, his voice had become brittle.

"Can you people here not see that the whites are deceiving you? For my part, I will never put any confidence in them.

Look around you. How well have you been treated by them? How much have you gained by the treaties you have signed in the absence of those who wished to save our land? As to you visiting chiefs here who sold to the white chief Harrison, the words I have to describe you, my mouth is too ashamed to speak. Dogs and skunks have not so little mind as those who did this. If only I had been here, not one inch of our land would have been bought. And every Indian who put his thumb to it should have his thumbs cut off!"

Tecumseh looked at them contemptuously and then strode through them, their bodies parting to let him pass. He did not look back and his nephew knew he would never come here again. Spemica Lawba felt shamed for his own people generally and for Catahecassa in particular and once again he wondered in his own heart if the course he had chosen was the correct one.

CHAPTER XXV

August 15, 1810

HE CONFRONTATION that occurred yesterday between the two giants — Tecumseh and Harrison — was an encounter that left everyone, including Harrison himself, more than a little shaken. It was the first time Spemica Lawba had ever seen any indication of fear manifest itself in the white leader. Now, in the early morning light, Spemica Lawba was wondering what would happen at this point, since an outbreak of war seemed imminent.

The governor had finally realized that the Americans had never before faced a greater potential threat than the one presented by Tecumseh. He knew now, unequivocally, that Tenskwatawa, as The Prophet, was merely a front for the far more dangerous Tecumseh. That was when Harrison had written about Tecumseh to Secretary of War Eustis:

> . . . *The implicit obedience and respect which the followers of Tecumseh pay to him is really astonishing and more than any other circumstance bespeaks him one of those uncommon geniuses which spring up occasionally to produce revolutions and overturn the established order of things. If it were not for the vicinity of the United States, he would perhaps be the founder of an empire that would rival in glory that of Mexico and Peru. No difficulties deter him. His activity and industry*

supply the want of letters. For four years he has been in constant motion. You see him today on the Wabash and in a short time you hear of him on the shores of Lake Erie, or Michigan, or the banks of the Mississippi, and wherever he goes he makes an impression favorable to his purpose. . . .

Harrison had also written to Tecumseh in Tippecanoe, inviting him to come to Vincennes to discuss their differences and perhaps settle them. At first Tecumseh had not been inclined to accept, but then decided he should make one final effort to make Harrison realize the need for him to return to the Indians all title to the three million acres of Indiana Territory he had so fraudulently purchased.

Tecumseh had come to Grouseland yesterday with a large entourage, but the council with Harrison had not gone at all well. Spemica Lawba and Winnemac were on hand as interpreters and stood behind and slightly to one side of Harrison, who sat on a straight chair. Tecumseh, with his Indians seated on the ground behind him, stood some twenty feet from Harrison and refused even to look at his nephew. He lost no time launching into his speech.

"Brother, I wish you to listen to me well. As I think you do not clearly understand what I before said to you, I will explain it again. Brother, since the peace was made, you have killed some of the Shawnees, Winnebagoes, Delawares and Miamis and you have taken our lands from us and I do not see how we can remain at peace if you continue to do so. *You* try to force the red people to do some injury. It is *you* that are pushing them on to do some mischief. You endeavor to make distinctions: you wish to prevent the Indians doing as we wish them — to unite and consider their lands as the common property of the whole; you take tribes aside and advise them not to come into this measure; and until our design is accomplished, we do not wish to accept your invitation to go and see the President. The reason I tell you this: you want, by your distinctions of Indian tribes in allotting to each a particular tract of land, to make them war with one another. You never see an Indian come, do you, and endeavor to make the white people do so? You are continually driving the red people; when, at last, you will drive them into the Great Lake, where they can't either stand or walk.

"Brother, you ought to know what you are doing with the Indians. Perhaps it is by direction of the President to make these distinctions. It is a very bad thing and we do not like it. Since my residence at Tippecanoe, we have endeavored to level all distinctions — to destroy village chiefs, by whom all mischief is done." He flicked his eyes briefly to Winnemac, who shifted uneasily. "It is they," Tecumseh continued, "who sell our lands to the Americans. Our object is to let our affairs be transacted by warriors.

"Brother, this land that was sold and the goods that were given for it were only done by a few. The treaty was afterwards brought here and the Weas were induced to give their consent, because of their small numbers. The treaty at Fort Wayne was made through the threats of Winnemac . . ." he now glared at the Potawatomi village chief, and Winnemac dropped his eyes, ". . . but in the future we are prepared to punish those chiefs who may come forward to propose to sell the land." Tecumseh returned his gaze to the governor. "If you continue to purchase them, it will produce war among the different tribes and, at last, I do not know what the consequences will be to the white people."

Referring to the letter Harrison had written to him, Tecumseh continued.

"Brother, you said if we could show you that the land was sold by people who had no right to sell, you would restore it." He pointed a level finger at Winnemac. "Those that did sell did not own it. These tribes set up a claim, but," he let his pointing arm swing toward the river where the majority of his warriors were waiting, "the tribes with me will not agree with their claim. If the land is not restored to us, you will see, when we return to our homes, how it will be settled. *Hear me!*" The two words exploded from him like rifle shots and Harrison jerked with surprise. "We shall have a great council at which all the tribes will be present, when we shall show to those who sold, that they had no right to the claim that they set up." Again his stare impaled Winnemac. "And we will see what will be done to those chiefs that did sell land to you."

Tecumseh placed his clenched fist to his chest. "I am not alone in this determination; it is the determination of all the warriors and red people that listen to me. I now wish *you*," his eyes flashed to Harrison, "to listen to me. If you do not, it will appear as if you wished to kill all the chiefs that sold you the land. I tell you so because I am authorized by all the tribes to do so. *I* am the head of them all! I am a warrior and the warriors will meet together and call for those chiefs that sold you the land and we shall know what to do with them. If you do not restore the land, you will have a hand in killing them!"

Winnemac paled, becoming suddenly very much afraid as he realized that this was no longer a vague threat. Some murmuring began in the assemblage but ceased at a gesture from Harrison, who then nodded at Tecumseh to continue.

"Brother, do not believe that I came here to get presents from you. If you offer us any, we will not take them. By our taking goods from you, you will hereafter say that with them you purchased another piece of land from us."

A flush appeared on the neck and cheeks of Harrison as the uncomfortable truth of what Tecumseh was saying struck home. Again he realized with forceful impact that the man he faced here was no ordinary Indian; that here was a man of intellect and rare power and ominous capability. Tecumseh, at the same time, was studying Harrison and abruptly realized that quite probably no matter what words were used on this man, it would make no difference, so he concluded his remarks quickly.

"Brother, I have declared myself freely to you and if any explanations should be required from our town, send a man who can speak to us." His eyes flicked for an instant toward Spemica

Lawba, then back to the governor. "As we intend to hold our council at the Huron village that is near the British, we may probably make them a visit; but should they offer us gunpowder and the tomahawk, we will take the powder and refuse the tomahawk. I wish you, brother, to consider everything I have said as true and that it is the sentiment of all the red people that listen to me."

When Tecumseh took his place with his people, Harrison came to his feet and began to speak. He denied that the Indians were one people and insisted that the Miamis had acted in their own best interest in selling the lands and that Tecumseh was not justified in trying to dictate whether or not the Miamis sold their own land. He turned to sit down and allow time for interpretation, but Tecumseh had understood his words and it became one of the rare occasions in his life where he lost his temper. He leaped to his feet, shouting loudly in the Shawnee tongue and gesticulating wildly.

"You are a liar! Everything you have said is false! The Indians have been cheated and imposed upon by you and by the Seventeen Fires. Nothing you have said, before or now, at this council, can be trusted. You lie and you cheat!"

For an instant disaster hung in the balance. Soldiers brought their guns to ready and weapons leaped into the hands of the assembled Indians. Only the sudden lifting of Harrison's hand in an unspoken command to stop prevented a bloody conflict. The frozen moment thawed and Harrison gradually lowered his arm. He looked at Spemica Lawba and spoke tightly.

"What did Tecumseh say, Johnny?"

As Spemica Lawba interpreted accurately, Harrison's face became pinched with constrained anger. "I will have no further communication with you," he told Tecumseh coldly. "You and your people may go in safety, since you have come under my protection to the council fire, but you must leave immediately."

At once Tecumseh and his party withdrew to their camp just outside Vincennes. By this time his temper had cooled and he was upset at himself for losing control, knowing it was just the sort of edge Harrison wanted in order to bring war down upon them. It was too soon for such a war to begin; it would damage the grand plan that had been in preparation for so many years. Much as he disliked it, he knew he would have to make amends.

Now, in the early morning sunlight, Spemica Lawba was considering yesterday's events and wondering where matters would lead from this point. He was clad in white man's shirt and trousers, but he wore moccasins and there was a sheathed knife at his belt. It was while he was pondering the situation that an Indian runner he did not recognize ran up and halted before him.

"I come from Tecumseh," he said, breathing heavily. "He wishes you to come to him at once."

"Does he wish this to be secret?" Spemica Lawba asked.

The runner shook his head vigorously. "No."

"Then wait. I will return to you in a moment."

In his identity as Johnny Logan, he went immediately to the mansion and presented himself to the governor, who was giving instructions to an army major. When Harrison learned of the summons, he nodded his head slowly.

"All right, go see what he wants, Johnny. But, if he wishes to renew the council fire, you may tell him that I will not tolerate any other insult from him such as yesterday's." His eyes glittered menacingly. "And you may tell him as well that while I do not want war with him and his people, I will not turn away if it comes to that."

Johnny Logan acknowledged and turned away, rejoined the runner and went with him directly to Tecumseh's camp. Within a quarter hour he was before him, looking him full in the eyes.

"Uncle?" he said.

Tecumseh barely inclined his head in recognition. "I first tell you," he said, "that your mother is well. She is with Tenskwatawa and Kumskaka in our Tippecanoe village."

"I am glad she is well." Spemica Lawba said nothing more, waiting.

Tecumseh let a heavy breath escape his lips. "I wish you to

carry to Governor Harrison my words of regret over what took place yesterday. Tell him I ask that the council be reconvened, that I may explain to him why I acted as I did. Assure him that no direct threat was intended against the whites attending the council and that such an action will not happen again."

"He would not tolerate it," the younger man said.

Tecumseh nodded briefly. "I know."

They were silent a moment and then the nephew said, "I will do as you ask," and turned to leave.

"Spemica Lawba!" When the younger man stopped and looked back, Tecumseh went on, his voice softened. "We miss you — your mother and your uncles. It is not too late for you and Pskipahcah Ouiskelotha and your sons to return to us."

A faint smile appeared on Spemica Lawba's lips. "I thank you. Pskipahcah Ouiskelotha is in the village of our chief, Catahecassa, where she cares for our two sons. She remains loyal to her chief, as do I. He *is* my chief, Tecumseh, and I will remain loyal to his wishes. Only if he should agree to join you — or should you come back to the Shawnees — can we be together again."

"Catahecassa *will* not," his uncle replied. "I cannot."

"Then it is sad," Spemica Lawba said softly.

"Yes," Tecumseh repeated, "it is sad." Abruptly he held out his hand and, surprised, his nephew gripped it with both of his and a wave of emotion rose in him. He dipped his head and raced away, tears having sprung into his eyes. He was convinced in his own heart that he had just shared with Tecumseh the last moment of intimacy they would ever have.

Less than an hour later, when Tecumseh arrived at the council ground adjacent to Grouseland, he saw that all the whites were heavily armed, but he did not comment on it. He faced Harrison and it was the governor who spoke without preamble.

"Do you intend to prevent the survey of the land on the Wabash?"

"I am determined that the old boundary shall continue."

As the governor looked in their direction, one by one the Indians among his following who had been chiefs in their own tribes came to their feet and stated their intention to support Tecumseh, saying that he was now their leader and they had all united as Indians. As the last chief finished, Harrison addressed Tecumseh.

"Since you have been candid in acknowledging your intentions, I would be so, too. I will send the President a faithful statement of what you have said in disputing the claims to the lands in question. I will tell you what the President's answer is when I receive it. However, I am sure that the President will never admit these lands to be the property of any other than those tribes who have occupied them since the white people came to America. Since we have come to title of them by fair purchase, then I am sure that these titles will be protected and supported by the sword."

"It would be only with great reluctance that I would make war upon the United States," Tecumseh responded. "However, if the President does not comply with my terms, I will be obliged to take the other side."

Harrison expelled a huge breath and repeated what he said before. "I will tell the President of your propositions. But again I say, there is not the least probability that he will accede to your terms."

"Well," Tecumseh said, gravely nodding, "as the great white chief is to determine the matter, I hope the Great Spirit will put sense enough in his head to induce him to direct you to give up this land. It is true, he is so far off he will not be injured by the war; he may sit in the town and drink his wine, while you and I will have to fight it out."

And William Henry Harrison could only nod.

CHAPTER XVI

November 18, 1811

SKIPAHCAH OUISKELOTHA had never before seen her husband so morose. A pall of gloom overhung him on his arrival home that immediately infected her and their sons and then soon expanded its influence to affect the whole population of Wapatomica. She knew what caused it, of course — they all knew in a very general way — but they did not know the details. Now, from Spemica Lawba, they would find out.

She brought him a fairly large pottery bowl filled with *succatash* and watched, pleased, as he wolfed it down, knowing he had not eaten anything but parched corn and bits of jerky for the past several days. Brimming with questions, she managed to hold her tongue until he had finished eating. She brought him his pipe, freshly packed with *kinnikinnick*, and then a glowing stick with which to light it. Not until he was puffing on it and more relaxed did she open the door to what had occurred.

"The battle at Tippecanoe . . .," she said hesitantly, ". . . it has finished Tecumseh?"

He shook his head. "It has finished Tenskwatawa. It has finished Tippecanoe. It has finished Tecumseh's great plan. But it has not finished Tecumseh. My uncle will never be finished until he breathes his final breath."

"We . . . we heard about the battle," she said. "Soon after.

No one knew exactly what happened. Only that it had. Poor Tecumseh. After all these years . . ." Her words dwindled away.

He nodded. "What he has lost cannot be recovered. He can only make the best of what he has left, but it is very little. I do not like Governor Harrison so much as I once did, but I respect him as a soldier even more. He is a very wise general and, as such, he took advantage of the only opportunity possible."

Her brow wrinkled. "I do not understand, Spemica Lawba. Will you tell me what happened?"

"I will tell you. Tecumseh's plan, which you understand in part from things I have told you in the past, was all but complete. He had only to visit a few of the southern tribes one final time. As before, he left Tenskwatawa in charge of Tippecanoe during his absence, with instructions to absolutely avoid any sort of conflict with the whites, or do anything that would give the whites an excuse to march against them. Even should the whites march against them in his absence, Tecumseh told Tenskwatawa, Tippecanoe should be abandoned and their people should melt away in the forests and gather again later. In that way nothing would be lost but the village itself, and wegiwas could easily be rebuilt."

"But Tenskwatawa failed Tecumseh?" she prompted as he paused.

"He failed in every way possible to fail," Spemica Lawba gritted. "And in the worst possible way, causing many Indians to die for no reason at all."

She waited silently, knowing he would continue when he was ready. And he did. For long hours he spoke to her, thoroughly and with the skill of the tribal story-tellers, chronologically putting together the pieces of a tragic mosaic.

"I feel I am partly to blame," Spemica Lawba had told her as he began his narration, "because of pieces of information that little birds brought to my ears, which I innocently relayed to Governor Harrison. What I told him was not significant, but when put together with the information he received from his large company of other spies, he began to realize the extent of my uncle's great plan. He also learned how soon that plan would ripen and fall upon him. It was then that Harrison became obsessed as I had never before seen him become: obsessed with a need to strike before it was too late. He was convinced, beyond my power to dissuade him, that the plan would work exactly as Tecumseh predicted. And he knew as well that the entire United States Army had not the fifth part of the warriors that Tecumseh's great sign would bring together; a force the army could not possibly stand against. The only thing he did not know was what the great sign would be. That was of little moment: he did not discount it and his fear was such as I had never expected to see in him — as was his determination to disrupt it while there was still time."

Carefully, missing no detail, Spemica Lawba continued his story, telling her how the only answer as Harrison saw it, was to demolish Tecumseh's incredible influence among the many tribes. If this could be done, then perhaps when — or if — the sign actually did come, the Indians Tecumseh expected would not come. Exactly *how* to do it was the knotty problem. He could not merely mount an army and attack. Not only had the President strictly forbidden such a move, there was no guarantee of success. In fact, failure was far more likely. Tecumseh's reputation as a formidable fighter and leader was not to be taken lightly. The answer, Harrison realized, lay in locating Tecumseh's Achilles' heel, his point of greatest vulnerability, and concentrating on it.

Ironically, it was through a slip of his own tongue that Tecumseh had provided Harrison his opportunity. The Achilles' heel of Tecumseh was a megalomanic brother who fancied himself The Prophet. After leaving Tenskwatawa in charge of Tippecanoe, with instructions on how to react to emergency situations, Tecumseh had set off in July with a small group of followers, stopping at Vincennes at Harrison's request for another council. Nothing of significance was decided, which was no surprise to either Tecumseh or Harrison, but it was in Tecumseh's final comments before his departure that the governor found the key he had hoped for.

"There is no point in speaking further with you here," Tecumseh had said. "I am leaving this country to visit the tribes to the south and ask them to become a part of our Indian nation. A great number of Indians will be coming back to settle on the Tippecanoe with us. We will make them welcome. But the land you falsely purchased on the Wabash is our finest hunting ground and we will need it to secure food for these people." Tecumseh caught himself, seeming suddenly to have realized his error. Immediately he sought to correct it and had continued in a stern voice. "I hope that nothing will be done by the whites toward settling this hunting ground before my return next spring."

Harrison had detected Tecumseh's mistake and successfully masked his jubilation until the Indians were gone. The key had been Tecumseh's revelation that he was going to the southern tribes again. The hastily added comment that he would return "next spring" was, Harrison was sure, merely a false trail in an effort to build a sense of complacency in the whites in a belief they had until next spring to prepare. Harrison knew that couldn't be true. His spies had reported that the red sticks Tecumseh had given the various chiefs all indicated that the great sign would come in December.

"Governor Harrison," Spemica Lawba went on as his wife listened intently, "had specific orders from his President that he could not attack the Indians, but that he could defend himself if attacked. So he knew that somehow he had to provoke the Tippecanoe Indians into attacking him. He also knew that Tecumseh would be far too shrewd to be maneuvered into such a position, but Tenskatawa was not. He had to make Tenskwatawa attack him before Tecumseh returned."

"But how could he do that?" Pskipahcah asked.

An expression of revulsion passed across her husband's face.

"The so-called Prophet opened the door for that," he said. "He sent a small party of the Tippecanoe Indians to steal some horses from isolated settlements near Vincennes. That, of itself, was not justification for Harrison to attack Tippecanoe, but the governor didn't think Tenskwatawa would be smart enough to realize that and he was right. He quickly mounted his army and marched them north in what he called 'merely a show of strength,' but fully aware that Tenskwatawa would not believe the army had no intention of attacking."

Spemica Lawba shook his head sadly and then went on to tell how Harrison's ploy had worked perfectly. The army had marched to within sight of the Tippecanoe campfires and camped. Despite the fact that Chaubenee, Wasegoboah and even Spemica Lawba's own mother had pleaded with Tenskwatawa not to attack, The Prophet would not listen and even threatened them with death if they continued to oppose him.

"He pretended to go into a trance," the Shawnee said, "and, in view of everyone at Tippecanoe, gave the impression that the Great Spirit was addressing the Indians through his lips. He convinced them that they could not be killed, that the whites could not fight at night and that any balls fired at them would pass through them without doing any harm; and he convinced them to attack just before dawn. They did, and Harrison was ready, with three cannon as well as his army. Once the attack was launched against him, Harrison took the offensive. It was a terrible slaughter."

For a long while, during which time he refilled and relighted his pipe, Spemica Lawba was quiet, but then he continued, telling Pskipahcah Ouiskelotha of the devastation to the Indians that had been the result of the Battle of Tippecanoe. During the battle Tenskwatawa had fled, but he was captured by Chaubenee, Roundhead and Wasegoboah and held prisoner for Tecumseh to deal with when he returned. Only a short while after the battle, Tecumseh *had* returned.

"And he killed Tenskwatawa?" Pskipahcah Ouiskelotha asked,

a tinge of expectancy in her words. It was evident she approved the execution of such a traitor to Tecumseh specifically and the Indians in general. But Spemica Lawba shook his head.

"No. But he did what he felt was worse. He banished him forever, telling him that for the rest of his life he would live outside Indian society, reviled by the very Indians he sought to rule, and that when at last he finally died, no living thing would mourn his death."

The two were silent for a long while and then Pskipahcah Ouiskelotha placed her hand on his forearm. "So now what happens?" she asked. "Has Tecumseh lost everything? What will he do now?"

"He has lost a great deal," Spemica Lawba admitted. "The majority of those who survived the battle scattered to their own homes, carrying word of the disaster with them. My uncle's prestige has suffered badly as the news of the defeat has reached the various villages and tribes. The Indians who have promised to support them will probably not do so now. They cannot be blamed for asking 'If Tecumseh cannot control his little brother, how can we then put our faith in him?' " He shrugged in that familiar manner and went on. "He still has those with him who would not have left him under any circumstances — Wasegoboah, my mother, my uncle Kumskaka, Chaubenee, Sauganash, Roundhead, others . . . but they are few."

"But what will he do?" she asked again.

"He has no choice at this point," Spemica Lawba told her softly, "except to go to the British and offer to them what strength he has remaining. It was something he wanted never to do, yet now he must. But he still has hope."

"Hope?" she echoed the word as a question. "How can he still have hope?"

"The great sign he has predicted for eleven years is still to come," he said. "A few days ago the green star burned its way across the sky. The last throw-away red stick has been thrown away by the chiefs of the tribes and the final stick has been cut into thirty lengths, with one such length being burned each day at dawn. If Tecumseh's great sign still comes at the time he predicted, those who still believe in him may rise and come to him and he could still rebuild what he has lost."

Silence filled the wegiwa for a considerable while. Pskipahcah Ouiskelotha had lowered her head as her husband had made his final comment. When at last she looked up, there was concern in her eyes.

"Will there be a war?" she whispered.

Spemica Lawba had asked this same question of William Henry Harrison less than a week ago and Harrison had replied that he was sure there would be, with the British as well as with the Indians, before next summer was upon them. The spy that Harrison knew as Johnny Logan now enfolded Pskipahcah Ouiskelotha in his arms and his reply was so soft it was almost inaudible.

"Yes. Soon."

CHAPTER XVII

December 16, 1811

 N THE MIDDLE of the night a large number of chiefs in widely scattered villages, from the Rocky Mountains to the Atlantic and from Canadian wilds to the Gulf of Mexico, burned the thirtieth piece of wood from the final red stick that each had cut up. They waited, as they had waited a month before when the great meteor had scorched the skies. For those far to the east the wait was two and a half hours; for those in the plains far west of the Mississippi it was an hour less. They waited for the sign first predicted eleven years ago by Tecumseh for this night.

At 2:30 A.M., a massive earthquake occurred where one had never happened before in recorded history; where no one could possibly have anticipated it; where no one could possibly have predicted it would strike.

No one except Tecumseh.

The area of the epicenter was where the great Ohio River empties into the greater Mississippi, the area where lands converged that were eventually to be known as Missouri, Illinois, Arkansas, Kentucky and Tennessee. Significantly, there were few humans in this immediate area and even fewer structures, so damage to man and his possessions was slight. But, in a monumental crescendo of sound beyond that which any living person had heard, the earth buckled and was split and torn.

Several miles from the Mississippi, along the border of Kentucky and Tennessee, a large section of ground caved in upon itself as if some incredibly heavy invisible foot had stepped on soft earth there crushing it. Water from subterranean sources gushed up, filling the depression and forming what would one day be called Reelfoot Lake. Great bluffs overlooking the midsection of the Mississippi River cracked and toppled and fell with horrendous grinding roar and splash into seething waters. For a time in this area, the river itself stopped and then flowed backward, flooding vast areas of lowland to great depth in some places, while riverbeds were lifted high and exposed in others. For many miles in a concentric circle from the epicenter the shock waves rolled out and the earth heaved and rolled and bucked as if it were a heavy fluid.

Settlers within a hundred miles were tossed from their beds as their cabins and barns splintered and crashed and bricks were ground into rubble in clouds of choking dust. Fires broke out. Bridges dropped into the rivers they spanned. Ravines filled with slipping earth and chasms appeared as the earth's crust split and separated with monumental thunderings. Birds shrieked and flapped as the trees in which they were roosting toppled in the darkness. Cattle and horses screamed in terror and were thrown to the ground. In all directions the effects were felt to varying degrees.

Such was the great sign that had been foretold so many years ago and continually during the years since. Though most of the warriors of widely separated tribes remained in their villages, there were those who picked up their weapons and began their journey toward the mouth of the Detroit River which, since the destruction of Tippecanoe, had become the new rendezvous for joining the force under an incredible Shawnee Indian.

Tecumseh.

CHAPTER XXVIII

July 29, 1812

I T WAS ONLY with difficulty that Spemica Lawba hid his extreme dislike of the American general.

In response to the summons from General William Hull, the Shawnee strode into the commander's Detroit headquarters and found him busily writing. Hull looked up and immediately his face became an ineffectual mask meant to hid his fear. Despite the fact that Johnny Logan was considered his most skilled and valuable guide, courier and spy, Hull still feared him. It was not surprising. General Hull was deeply afraid of *all* Indians.

"Take a seat, Mr. Logan," the general said, indicating a straight chair against the far wall, "while I finish here."

Spemica Lawba did as bade, watching as the officer dipped his quill pen and resumed writing. He wondered, as he had wondered a hundred times or more since late May, how such an ineffectual man could possibly have been chosen as commander of the Northwestern Army of the United States.

Until late last winter, William Hull had been governor of the Michigan Territory. With the possibility of war with England looming ever closer, he had been called to the nation's capital, given a leave of absence from his gubernatorial duties, and appointed commander of the Northwestern Army, with Major

General Henry Dearborn, former Secretary of War, named as commanding general of all United States forces. Hull was ordered to go to Ohio at once, build up an army as quickly as possible, and march it to Detroit. If and when war actually broke out, he was immediately to cross the Detroit River and invade Canada.

Hull gathered his army, first at Cincinnati, then at Dayton and finally at Urbana, Ohio, from which point the march northward through the wilderness was to begin. By this time Indian outbreaks were occurring all throughout the northwest, especially in the Illinois and Indiana territories. It had been at Urbana that Spemica Lawba, under instructions from Governor Harrison, had joined Hull's force to guide it to Detroit and equally to serve as courier, adviser and spy to the general. The fact that William Hull blanched and recoiled every time Johnny Logan came anywhere near him had not encouraged any sort of friendship to develop between them, although the Shawnee's skill did generate a grudging respect in the general.

The army, with Spemica Lawba guiding, left Urbana in early June and marched up through Shawnee country — where Chief Catahecassa's warriors were remaining neutral — to the Maumee River, where, after building some forts en route, they arrived June 30. Already Hull had become something of a laughingstock to the two thousand men serving beneath him; the frequent butt of coarse jokes and crude frontier humor. No one realized yet that matters had gone beyond the funny stage.

On June 18, the United States had declared war on Great Britain.

Though this had long been planned by the government, no one thought to inform the commander of the Northwestern Army until the declaration of war had become a *fait accompli*. It was a grievous oversight, belatedly rectified only on the day of the declaration when notification of it was sent to Hull — addressed to him at Detroit — in an ordinary mail packet instead of by express rider, despite everyone's awareness that ordinary mail packets often took an inordinate time to be delivered, providing they were not lost en route, which frequently happened.

At the Maumee, Hull hired a schooner — the *Cuyahoga* — to transport the heavy baggage, excess arms, musicians and their instruments, and thirty ailing officers and soldiers to Detroit by water. Some of his officers objected, pointing out that war was imminent and that the ship would have to sail right past the British Fort Malden at Amherstburg immediately after entering the Detroit River. Hull had sloughed off their fears, stating that he would be informed well in advance if war was to be declared. The commander's son, Captain Abraham Hull, in a rare effort to be helpful during one of the few periods he was not drunk, considerately included in the baggage loaded aboard the schooner a trunk containing all of the army's field reports, war plans, muster roles, supply and armament lists and invasion plans.

When Spemica Lawba, after a scout into the enemy territory, discovered that Tecumseh and over two thousand of his followers were hovering on both sides of the Detroit River as active allies to the British, Hull actually began trembling with his fear and it took him some time to calm down. With the schooner on its way, the march was resumed up the west shore of Lake Erie toward Detroit.

At last someone in the nation's capital realized that somebody ought to check and see if the letter to Hull, advising him that war had been declared, had ever reached its destination. It hadn't. A frantic search resulted in it finally being located in a mail pouch at Cleveland. Immediately it was dispatched by express rider to Hull. That rider reached the Maumee the day after Hull's departure and followed, finally catching up and delivering the important document on July 2. Hull was stunned and immediately sent out a detachment to aid the *Cuyahoga* if possible, but it was too late. British communications being much better than American, the garrison at Fort Malden had some time before been apprised that a state of war existed between England and the United States. Thus, when the schooner appeared, it was boarded and all aboard were made prisoners of war. The *Cuyahoga* was then taken as a prize of war to the Amherstburg port . . . along with all Hull's war plans and other military papers. In his tardy concern over the safety of the ship and its contents, human and otherwise, General Hull neglected to inform the American commanders at either Fort Wayne or Fort Mackinac that war had been declared.

The tragic comedy of errors continued. The army, having successfully avoided encountering the enemy due to Johnny Logan's skillful guiding, reached Detroit on July 5. Johnny was dispatched to spy out the enemy forces and reported back quickly that the British had only about two hundred soldiers at Amherstburg and that mass desertion of most of the militia had occurred at the approach of Hull's army. All factors were ideal for an immediate invasion, but Hull vacillated. For a week he held his impatient army in Detroit before finally crossing over the Detroit River, unopposed, on July 12 and occupying the Canadian town of Sandwich. A few detachments were sent out, captured important supplies on the Thames River, then had a skirmish with the enemy at the crucial Canard River bridge and gained control of it. The way was now clear for a drive against Fort Malden, only four miles south, but Hull, incomprehensibly, ordered the detachment back and the enemy regained control of the bridge. At the same time, one of Hull's aides was seen going to the enemy under a white flag. Hull, at the demands of his field officers to explain this, insisted he knew nothing about it. Almost immediately, leaving his army without definite orders or explanation, Hull abruptly recrossed the Detroit River by himself. No one knew when — or even *if* — he intended to return.

On July 17, not having been informed of the war, the American commander of Fort Mackinac awoke to find his fortification surrounded by a British and Indian force from St. Joseph Island. During the night the enemy's artillery had been positioned on the cliffs overlooking the fort. Surrender being demanded, he had no choice but to capitulate without a shot being fired. Hull had finally come back to the Canadian side of the river and rejoined his army on July 26. Very shortly afterward a British ship arrived from the north and disgorged its load of American prisoners — the garrison of Fort Mackinac. Hull was appalled at the disaster and envisioned hordes of Indians sweeping down from the north against him. Further, the British takeover of Mackinac had effectively cut the American supply line to Fort Dearborn at Chicago.

Morale in Hull's army was dangerously low, but it improved considerably when he posted an order for a full assault against Fort Malden to take place. At last the army was to have its chance to fight! Men and supplies were loaded into boats and then, at the moment of casting off, Hull ordered the whole force to Detroit. The army was thunderstruck and whispers of mutiny began circulating.

That was the situation now — the humiliated Northwestern Army of the United States bottled up at the fort in Detroit and its frightened commander writing dispatches, while reports were circulating of a strong British reinforcement on its way to Fort Malden.

With a flourish and a sign, General Hull signed the second letter, addressed its envelope to Captain Nathan Heald, Commanding at Fort Dearborn, and then lay down his pen and read over what he had written:

SIR: —

   It is with regret I order the evacuation of your post owing to the want of provisions only a neglect of the Commandant of Fort Mackinac has occasioned.
   You will, therefore, destroy all arms and ammunition, but

*the goods of the factory you may give to the friendly Indians
who may be desirous of escorting you on to Fort Wayne and to
the poor and needy of your post.*

*I am informed this day that Mackinac and the island of St.
Joseph will be evacuated on account of the scarcity of provision
and I hope in my next to give you an acct. of the Surrender of
the British at Malden as I expect 600 men here by the beginning of September.*

Wm. Hull, Commd Gen.

The fact that his order to Captain Heald at Fort Dearborn
was couched in lies bothered General Hull not at all. He gave a
little grunt of satisfaction, folded the letter, and sealed it inside
the envelope, then came to his feet. Spemica Lawba rose also.
He watched as the general slipped the envelope into a larger
envelope, also containing a folded letter, addressed to Captain
Rhea, commander of Fort Wayne, and then sealed that one as
well. The covering letter to Rhea explained briefly about the
evacuation order and instructed him to relay the enclosed letter
for Captain Heald to Fort Dearborn by the swiftest means possible. Rhea was also instructed to render to Captain Heald any
assistance it was in his power to give.

"Mr. Logan," Hull said, handing Spemica Lawba the bulky
envelope, "you are the most capable person we have here for
this mission. I want you to leave here at once and deliver this
only into the hands of Captain Rhea at Fort Wayne."

"I will get it there, General," Spemica Lawba said.

General Hull had no doubt whatever that he would.

CHAPTER XXIX

August 2, 1812

NDIAN RUNNER ouside, Captain," the corporal said, sticking his head inside Oscar James Rhea's office at Fort Wayne. "Looks pretty wore out. Says he's got a dispatch for you."

Rhea made no effort to hide the half-empty whiskey bottle gripped in his hand. With annoyed look, he set the bottle down on the desk and corked it. The noncommissioned officer remained at the door and Rhea snapped at him.

"Well, dammit, man, give it to me!"

"He wouldn't give it to me. He says he has to place it directly in your hands, sir, by order of General Hull."

That was unusual, and Rhea straightened. "All right, Corporal, send him in."

As the soldier ducked out, the Fort Wayne commander snugged the cork down a little tighter and put the bottle into a desk drawer. In a moment the noncom ushered Spemica Lawba into the room and stood waiting.

"You can leave, Corporal," Rhea said.

"Yes sir."

As the soldier exited, closing the door after him, Rhea squinted at Spemica Lawba and then smiled faintly. "I know you," he said. "You're Johnny Logan."

The Shawnee nodded and withdrew the envelope from his blouse, handing it to the commanding officer. "From General Hull at Detroit," he said.

Rhea broke the seal and withdrew the folded letter and another sealed envelope. He frowned as he read Hull's instructions and then picked up the sealed envelope and looked it over. "Corporal!" he bawled. The door opened quickly and Rhea flicked his hand at him. "Get word to Captain Wells and Winnemac to come here on the double."

In less than ten minutes the pair arrived. The Captain Wells turned out to be William Wells, now Indian agent at this post, whom Spemica Lawba knew very well as a fellow spy for Harrison, but with whom he had never formed any close friendship. Winnemac, too, was no stranger, but Spemica Lawba had never liked or trusted him. The two greeted him casually.

"Johnny just brought me a rather urgent dispatch from General Hull," Rhea said. He picked up the letter from his desk and read it aloud to them. There was immediate concern evident in Wells's expression. His niece, Rebekah, was at Fort Dearborn.

"I know of no better team to carry the order to Captain Heald than you and Winnemac, Captain," he said. "Assuming, of course, you're willing to undertake it. There could well be some jeopardy involved for you."

"Maybe," spoke up Winnemac. "Maybe not."

"There could be problems," Wells said slowly. "In fact, I'd bet on it, especially if Heald follows those orders to the letter. Obviously, General Hull doesn't understand the problem."

"What do you mean?"

"Captain, if they destroy all their excess weapons and ammunition and give away all their supplies and march out of the fort, they're asking for trouble. God only knows what might happen, but it's an open invitation to attack. You know the mischief the Indians have already done there; they massacred those people at the Lee Farm not four miles from Fort Dearborn last April."

"That attack was made by a party of Winnebagoes from the Fox River," Winnemac put in immediately, himself a Potawatomi like Black Partridge.

"That's what we've heard," Wells responded. "It may or may not be true. But I sure wouldn't count on Black Partridge giving them an escort to here. He's declared himself to Tecumseh. Isn't that true, Johnny?"

"It is true," Spemica Lawba replied.

"Well, I don't like it. Not at all." Wells shook his head and looked at the commander again. "Captain Heald's married to my niece and I know him, but not all that well. You probably know him better. What do you think his reaction will be when he gets the order?"

"I know exactly what he'll do," Rhea said without hesitation. "He'll follow it to the letter. It's an order from his commanding general, isn't it? He has no choice."

"Damn!" Wells turned to face the Potawatomi. "Winnemac, what do you think? Will Black Partridge's people give them an escort?"

Winnemac grunted sourly. "No escort," he said. "Bad birds are flying everywhere. I have been told they recently came to roost on Black Partridge's shoulder and whispered things into his ear."

"What if I brought an escort from here? Not soldiers. I mean some of the Miamis. Fifty or a hundred?"

Winnemac shrugged. "You would have a difficult time convincing any Miamis to act as escort. It would indicate that they are no longer neutral, that they are on the side of the Americans. The Potawatomies — Black Partridge, Siggenauk, Naunongee, Sunawewonee, Nescotnemeg, others — all would be very angry."

"You agree?" Wells asked Spemica Lawba.

"Yes. The Shawnees and Miamis have declared themselves neutral in this war. Some individuals might help, just as you and I help the Americans without our tribes committing themselves, but if fifty or a hundred went with you as escort, the Potawatomies might feel the Miami tribe as a whole has committed itself. It could bring problems."

"Maybe, but dammit, they wouldn't hit a hundred Miamis! There'd be hell to pay."

"*If* you could get them to go along with you," Winnemac said slowly, "they might not hit one hundred Miamis. They might not hit fifty. Less than fifty . . ." He left the sentence dangling and shrugged again.

"I'll get them," Wells said. "You're willing to go?"

"I would go," Winnemac said. "I would carry message. I would not be escort. I would not fight Potawatomi."

Wells grunted and turned to the commander. "All right, if it suits you, Captain, let's do it this way. Let's send Winnemac off with the message right away. He'll have no trouble getting through. They're his own people. I'll round up an escort of Miamis to follow as soon as possible. May take a few days, but I think we'll get there in time."

Rhea nodded. "Do it that way. I'll send Johnny here back with a dispatch for General Hull, telling him what we've done." He handed the sealed envelope to Winnemac. "Get this to Captain Heald as soon as you can." As Winnemac nodded, the commander turned to Wells. "I hope you'll get your niece back safely, Captain."

Wells grinned mirthlessly, signaled Winnemac with a jerk of his head, and then the pair were gone.

Again Spemica Lawba had to wait while a letter was written.

CHAPTER XXX

August 12, 1812

 PEMICA LAWBA had hoped matters would have improved for the Americans in the Detroit area by the time he got back, but they definitely had not.

Colonel Lewis Cass, one of the militia commanders, confessed that the only bright spot in their existence here at Detroit had been Spemica Lawba's return on August 9. No shred of confidence remained among the troops for their general, and with good cause. A supply convoy from Ohio under Captain Henry Brush had gotten only as far as the Raisin River at Frenchtown along Lake Erie's western shore, but so many of Tecumseh's Indians were between them and Detroit that they could not proceed farther without General Hull's dispatching a strong detachment to escort them in. Hull at first refused the request, but upon being confronted by his angry field officers, gave in and authorized Major Thomas van Horne to lead a detachment of one hundred eighty soldiers to the Frenchtown rendezvous and bring the convoy here with its crucial supplies.

They hadn't made it. In a brilliant maneuver planned by Tecumseh, the detachment had been ambushed at Brownstown the day before Spemica Lawba's return. Tecumseh had suffered a slight wound in the side from a rifle ball and Little Blue Jacket was killed and beheaded but, other than that, the disaster was entirely the Americans'. The detachment was forced to retreat back to Detroit with twenty men wounded, seventeen left dead at the scene of the ambush and seventy missing. That fight had been only a prologue.

A larger detachment under Hull's second-in-command was sent out — six hundred soldiers. Once again Tecumseh set up an ambush, this time with only seventy Indians and forty British soldiers. As they reached the site of Wyandot Chief Walk-in-the-Water's abandoned village, the ambush was sprung and a severe battle ensued. The Americans still held the battlefield when it was all over — giving Hull the excuse he needed to report a victory to the Secretary of War — but as one of the soldiers involved wrote, "*If that was a victory, I hope to God I never live to see a defeat!*" The statistics told the story much more accurately than Hull had. Two Indians were killed and six wounded. Six British soldiers had been killed and twenty-one wounded. But among the Americans there were eighteen dead and fifty-seven wounded.

For some time General William Hull's officers and men had considered him not only incompetent, but equally a fool and a coward. No one had any shred of confidence left in him. And now, because of what had happened only a short while ago, they considered him traitorous as well. One American, Robert Lucas, writing to a friend of his in Ohio, was extremely bitter, saying that there had never been a more patriotic army than the one he was in, nor one that had more completely the power in its grasp to have accomplished its aim; an army, he went on furiously, that had now sunk into disgrace because of its commanding general. He termed Hull imbecilic and treacherous and in every respect opposed to his colonels, and he yearned for one of them to take over and vindicate the army.

Spemica Lawba had been included in the secret meetings being held by the three Ohio militia colonels — Lewis Cass, Duncan MacArthur and James Findley. Those meetings came to a head today. Their consensus was that Hull was obviously incapable of properly commanding the army and was it therefore not their duty — ethically, if not officially — to remove him from power? A plan gelled and they carried it with some trepidation to Hull's second-in-command, a regular United States lieutenant colonel named James Miller, who they believed felt as strongly about the situation as they, even though he had not dared to be so vocal about it. If Cass, MacArthur and Findley forcibly removed Hull from command, would Miller then take command of the army? Miller weighed the consequences and then reluctantly shook his head. What they were suggesting was mutiny and it could result in a death penalty for him. But he turned the tables by offering to support the three colonels in a takeover if Duncan MacArthur would assume command of the army. Now it was MacArthur who backpedaled. They *knew* Hull was guilty of cowardice, incompetence and perhaps even treason, yet knowing it and proving it were two different matters and the death penalty was as real a threat to MacArthur as to Miller. He, too, declined.

It was decided to write a letter immediately to Governor Meigs of Ohio, in whom they all had great confidence, and state to him in couched terms what the situation was here. In subtle manner they would suggest placing command of the army in his hands if he came. Cass undertook the the actual writing of the letter, but Miller — giving his word to provide them verbal support — refused to put his signature to the letter. The colonels agreed and that was where Spemica Lawba and a soldier named Murray came into the picture. No courier was so skilled or more apt to get through the enemy lines with a message than Johnny Logan; and no other soldier available to go would be better able to fill in the between-the-lines situation than Murray. So as Johnny Logan and Murray waited, Cass wrote swiftly.

Detroit, August 12, 1812

Dear Sir:

From causes not fit to put upon paper, but which I trust I shall one day live to communicate to you, this army has been reduced to a critical and alarming situation. We have wholly left the Canadian shore, and have left the miserable inhabitants, who depended upon our will and our power to protect them, to their fate. Unfortunately, the General and the principal officers could not view our situation and our prospects in the same light. That Malden might easily have been reduced, I have no doubt. That the army were in force and spirits enough to have done it, no one doubts. But the precious opportunity has fled, and instead of looking back, we must now look forward.

The letter from the Secretary of War to you, a copy of which I have seen, authorizes you to preserve and keep open the communication from the State of Ohio to Detroit. It is all important it should be kept open. Our very existence depends upon it. Our supplies must come from our State. This country does not furnish them. In the existing state of things, *nothing but a large force of two thousand men at least, will effect the object. It is the unanimous wish of the army, that you should accompany them.*

Every exertion that can, must be made. If this reaches you safely by Murray, he will tell you more than I can or ought here to insert.

Very respectfully,
I am your's, &c.
Lewis Cass

The ink was not even dry when Quartermaster General James Taylor burst in with unbelievable news: a boat from the American side, bearing an officer, was moving across the river under a white flag, directly to the British position. Telling Murray and Johnny Logan to wait, MacArthur, Cass and Findley raced to Hull's office and indignantly demanded an explanation. Hull assumed a pretense of surprise and incomprehension that fooled no one. He said he would check on it at once and excused himself to query one of his aides, a Captain Hickman. In a few moments he returned and offhandedly told them that Hickman had had a conversation with Captain Rough on the matter of a capitulation of the American army. Hickman, Hull said, did not wish Captain Rough to consider that he had permission to carry a truce flag to the enemy. "However," he added lamely, "evidently Captain Rough probably misunderstood and believed he had such permission. That's all I know, gentlemen."

It was a dismissal, and the three Ohio colonels, containing their fury only with the greatest of difficulty, returned to the room where Johnny Logan and Murray still waited, along with James Taylor and Major Elijah Brush of the Michigan Territorial Militia. A postscript was now hastily added to the reverse side of the letter Cass had written a short while before:

> *Since the other side of this letter was written, new circumstances have arisen. The British force is opposite, and our situation has nearly reached its crisis. Believe all the bearer will tell you. Believe it, however it may astonish you, as much as if told you by one of us. Even a ———— is talked of by the— —— ————. The bearer will supply the vacancy. On you we depend.*
>
> > *Lewis Cass,*
> > *James Findley,*
> > *Duncan M'Arthur,*
> > *James Taylor,*
> > *E. Brush.*

Cass folded and sealed the letter in three places with wax. He placed it in a waterproof pouch and handed it to Murray. "There are three blanks in this letter," he told them. "Verbally fill them in when Governor Meigs reads this letter. The first is 'capitulation' and the remaining two are 'commanding officer.' "

The officers all shook hands with Murray and Johnny Logan in turn.

"We'll get the message through to Governor Meigs," Spemica Lawba said.

Cass looked at him soberly for a moment and then smiled faintly.

"If anyone can," he said, "it's you."

CHAPTER XXXI

August 13, 1812

PEMICA LAWBA stopped his horse so abruptly that Murray's ran into it. The soldier, clad in frontiersman's garb, opened his mouth in surprise, but before he could demand an explanation the Shawnee's hand was raised in a gesture of silence and the unspoken question died. Instantly, Murray was fearfully alert, mentally cursing himself for having, only a mile or so back, thrust his heavy rifle into the scabbard.

Even though they left Detroit under cover of darkness yesterday, the pair had been expecting to be cut off at every turn. They had traveled all night in a state of perpetual alertness but had successfully avoided any contact with the enemy. Now, well into the day and approaching the Ohio border, they were following a dim woodland trail and were so far off the principal route from the Maumee to Detroit that there was little reason to expect interception. It was just the barest flick of his horse's ear that had given Spemica Lawba warning, but even that had come too late.

Five mounted Indians, three with leveled rifles, moved out from behind a large outcropping of rock. The three with their weapons trained on the couriers were not familiar to Spemica Lawba but the other two were. One was his uncle, the other his stepfather — Tecumseh and Wasegoboah.

Tecumseh's expression was set in stern lines, Wasegoboah's was unreadable.

As Murray sat stiffly motionless in his saddle, wide-eyed and clutching the reins with white-knuckled intensity, Spemica Lawba dipped his head in recognition, first to his uncle, then to his stepfather.

"I have heard that you were wounded recently," he said in a conversational tone to Tecumseh. "I hope you have recovered well."

"It is of little significance, Spemica Lawba," Tecumseh replied. "Other matters are of much greater importance here. Where are you and this one with you going?"

Spemica Lawba had prepared for this eventuality. "We have been sent to speak with the Ohio governor," he said. "The army needs supplies, but those supplies have, as you know, been prevented from getting through. We are to request Governor Meigs that he send a detachment from below to escort that convoy through."

Tecumseh shook his head. "It is too late," he said. "Even should a large force be sent, it could not accomplish that mission."

Spemica Lawba knew Tecumseh was neither lying nor exaggerating, and a sliver of fear stabbed him. He wished he knew why his uncle was so definite in his statement. He was also thankful that Murray could not understand the Shawnee tongue and become even more afraid.

"We are enemies now, Spemica Lawba," said his stepfather. "You are a spy for the enemy. It is our place to kill you, as *we* would be killed if we were taken by the Americans. Long ago you made your choice against —"

"There will be no killing here, Wasegoboah," Tecumseh interrupted, his sternness evaporating. "Tecumapese had suffered loss of this son once already; there is no reason here to make her suffer the same loss twice. There has been killing enough and much more to come. The mission of these two is of no consequence to what will be at Detroit. We will let them pass."

"I am indebted to my uncle," Spemica Lawba said. "I hope my mother is well?"

"Tecumapese is well."

"I would ask that you tell her that her son and his wife are also well, as are her grandsons. Perhaps one day we may all be reunited."

"It will never be, Spemica Lawba. I will tell her, but I tell you now, our families will never be reunited. I also tell you this: you have chosen your side and I have chosen mine. We are both too much alike for either of us to change from the course our heart tells us to take. Our only great difference is that in choosing my path, I *know* it is the only one I can take. You, in choosing yours, still have doubts rising to assail you. This can only make sorrow your companion. You have made your choice. Now put all doubt aside and leave no room for regret. But know as well that what Wasegoboah said to you was true: now we are enemies. If again we should meet in such circumstance, either you must kill me or I will kill you."

"I understand, Tecumseh."

His uncle kneed his horse forward and came to a stop beside his nephew's. He reached out and squeezed Spemica Lawba's shoulder. "May Moneto go with you, nephew. Farewell."

He wheeled his horse around and galloped off, followed by Wasegoboah and the three warriors. In a short while even the sound of hoofbeats dwindled, swallowed up by the forest.

"God Almighty!" wheezed Murray, blowing out a great breath. "I don't know what you said to 'em, Johnny, but you sure saved our skins. Let's get the hell out of here!"

The Shawnee nodded and put his horse into motion southward, hearing Murray following. But his mind was not on Murray now, nor on their mission. It was on what Tecumseh had advised him: that having made his choice, he must put aside all doubt and have no regret.

But Spemica Lawba could not.

CHAPTER XXXII

September 10, 1812

INNEMAC, the Potawatomi, had at various times pledged loyalty to his own tribe, to William Henry Harrison, to William Wells, to the Americans, to the British, to the Indian cause generally and to Tecumseh in particular. In truth, he was an opportunist and, as such, wholly incapable of loyalty to any person or any cause. His one great concern in life was looking out for himself.

When he left Fort Wayne carrying the order from General Hull to Captain Nathan Heald for the evacuation of Fort Dearborn at Chicago, he began to realize that the fortunes of this war — which he had initially thought would be with the Americans — were leaning in the direction of the British and Indians. With this in mind, it only made sense to him to mend his fences somewhat where the foes of the Americans were concerned. He therefore stopped several times en route to Chicago and, having carefully opened Hull's order without destroying the seal, showed it to the Potawatomi chiefs. With this information they quickly put the finishing touches to their plan for attack. Winnemac continued to Chicago and delivered the resealed orders. Some days afterward William Wells showed up with thirty Miami warriors who had agreed to act as an escort. Wells and others at Chicago begged Heald not to destroy the arms and ammunition, not to turn over supplies to the Indians and most certainly not to abandon Fort Dearborn. He refused to listen. General Hull was his superior and had given him an order. He meant to follow that order . . . to the letter.

On August 15 the gates of Fort Dearborn were thrown open and the garrison marched out, along with the citizens of Chicago. Only a short distance from the fort the Potawatomies attacked, the Miami escort fled, and a terrible massacre of scores of Americans resulted. Among those killed was William Wells, who was shot, beheaded and his heart cut from his body and eaten.

On August 16, a terrified General William Hull, in opposition to his officers and with no good basis for so doing, surrendered the Northwestern Army of the United States to the British.

Now the humiliated United States government had named General James Winchester, who fancied himself a great strategist, as the new commander of the Northwestern Army, with Governor William Henry Harrison appointed brigadier general under him. That all the Americans on the frontier were sure the roles of these two men should have been reversed was obviously not a view shared by the President and Secretary of War.

Flushed with success, the Indians — acting in opposition to Tecumseh's recommendations — moved against Fort Wayne. Captain Oscar James Rhea and his garrison of seventy men were inside. Rhea, ineffectual commander at best, took refuge in a whiskey bottle. For over a week now, the Indians had kept the fort under siege and it was finally Winnemac who, last night, devised a clever plan for getting the gates open. Before dawn a large concentration of heavily armed warriors hid in a semicircle around two sides of the fort. The plan was that just after sunrise, Winnemac and four other chiefs draped in blankets would openly approach the fort under a flag of truce and ask to be permitted inside to discuss a peace proposal. When Captain Rhea had gathered his officers together, the five would suddenly pull the hidden pistols from under their blankets and kill the three lieutenants, sparing only the captain. Chief Winnemac knew only too well about the officer's alcoholism and believed him to be a weak man who, once his officers were dead and his own skin threatened, would agree to open the gates and surrender the fort.

Now, with the well-hidden Indians in position, Winnemac and the other four chiefs were ready. They started walking toward the fort under their white flag and had almost reached the bastion when two Shawnees and a white man rode up. The latter was William Oliver, one of General Harrison's foremost scouts. The two Shawnees with him were his friends of long standing, Bright Horn and Johnny Logan. They had come as an advance party to inform Rhea that Harrison, now a general, was already on the march for Fort Wayne with his army. They informed Winnemac of this, but not of the fact that it would take that force two or three days of marching at their regular pace to arrive here.

Winnemac shook hands sullenly with each of the three, suddenly fearful that Harrison was very close behind them, suddenly filled with the urgency to protect himself. He scowled and pretended to be angry.

"You have spoiled it! These chiefs," he indicated the equally scowling four with him, "were willing to talk peace. Now you come with an army at your heels and they have decided not to talk peace after all. Come," he told the other chiefs, "I will escort you back to your warriors."

They turned and walked away swiftly. As they reached the nearby woodland, firing broke out and the three scouts ducked into the fort. The firing continued at a high pitch, interspersed with flaming arrows that several times set the walls afire. The fires were quickly extinguished with kegs of water poured down the walls from the parapets. Rhea was so drunk he could barely stand and he was relieved by Lieutenant Joseph Curtis, who ordered him confined. Curtis then furnished every man able to shoot with several stands of weapons, ordering them to hold off firing until the enemy came close. The strategy worked well.

Evidently believing the garrison out of ammunition, the hordes of Indians rushed the place, only to fall back under withering fire, leaving eighteen of their number dead. It was heartening to the garrison. Nevertheless, unless someone got word to Harrison right away, the fort might well be taken.

"We'll go," said Johnny Logan quietly. "Teopah Kouleelawba and I will get through to General Harrison."

Curtis was dubious, but William Oliver spoke up. "If anyone can do it," he told the new commander, "Johnny Logan and Bright Horn can."

There was no time for discussion, and Lieutenant Curtis gave his approval. The pair were provided with fresh horses and at the next break in the firing they thundered out of the gate and swept past the enemy lines, barely ahead of the converging Indians, who were unmounted. As the riders galloped into the far woods, Johnny Logan raised his arm in a wave and gave a triumphant shout, echoed by a hearty cheer from the entire garrison.

CHAPTER XXXIII

September 12, 1812

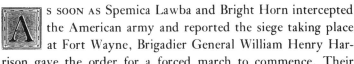S SOON AS Spemica Lawba and Bright Horn intercepted the American army and reported the siege taking place at Fort Wayne, Brigadier General William Henry Harrison gave the order for a forced march to commence. Their approach gave the attacking Potawatomi Indians one last opportunity to attempt a ruse that Winnemac had seen work on more than one occasion in his life.

First they built several large fires at a distance from Fort Wayne to give the impression to those inside that a hot battle was in progress. Then, in great disorder and acting the part of a routed force, they fled past the gates, just outside effective rifle range. The object was to make the garrison think the Indians were being pursued by Harrison and thereby draw them out to aid in that pursuit; whereupon the fleeing Indians would lead them directly into a devastating ambush. But just as Winnemac had seen such a ruse work before, so too had Captain Curtis, and he kept the garrison inside the fort.

Less than an hour later, Spemica Lawba and Teopah Kouleelawba emerged from the woods on their horses, followed in another few minutes by Harrison leading his army. A great cheer went up and the gates were thrown open. The siege was over and yet another disaster for the Americans was averted.

"I only hope that one day," Harrison told his men, "the United States will fully realize what a debt of gratitude it owes to Johnny Logan and the Shawnees. I intend to see to it."

And Spemica Lawba was very pleased.

CHAPTER XXXIV

November 25, 1812

T WAS LESS than three weeks ago when William Henry Harrison, still at Fort Wayne, summoned Spemica Lawba.

"I have another mission for you, Johnny," he told him. "It might be better if you didn't attempt this one alone. I'd suggest you select a couple of good men to go with you. I want you to do some spying on the enemy down toward the Rapids."

Johnny Logan nodded, already having decided that he would ask his two closest friends, Bright Horn and Otter, to accompany him.

The valley of the Maumee had become the arena for the frontier portion of the War of 1812 and, since losing Detroit to the British, the American toehold in this country was limited to two bastions — Fort Wayne at the convergence of the St. Joseph and St. Marys River, and Fort Winchester at the point where old Fort Defiance had once stood, where the Auglaize River emptied into the Maumee, halfway between Fort Wayne and Lake Erie. Fort Winchester had been named after General Winchester, who had overseen its construction. It was a dangerous post, with British agents and Indians constantly moving about in the woods, and soldiers who became careless were likely to end up a captive or dead.

The British and Indians were operating from a newly established camp at the lower end of the Maumee Rapids, where the old Fort Miami had once stood. But, while the Americans knew of their presence there, they did not know their plans. That was what Johnny Logan and his companions were to discover, if at all possible.

"It's a hazardous assignment, Johnny, and I want you to be extremely careful. But it's exactly *because* of the hazard involved that I don't know who would stand a better chance of getting the intelligence we need than you. Don't go downstream any farther than the foot of the Rapids, but reconnoiter whatever you can of the enemy's movements between there and Fort Winchester. If you can take a prisoner or two, so much the better. You don't need to come all the way back here to Fort Wayne. Report to Fort Winchester, directly to Winchester himself or, if he's not available, to his second-in-command, Major Price."

The three spies had set off immediately, spying from treetops or from under brush piles at the activities of the enemy. They gathered some few bits of interesting information, but Spemica Lawba was not satisfied.

"I want to do something else," he told Gituta and Teopah Kouleelawba at their fireless camp near a large encampment of Tecumseh's combined Indian forces, "but it will be very dangerous. I think the only way we are going to possibly learn anything about their future plans is for me to mingle with them and try to overhear what is being said."

Gituta grinned lopsidedly at Teopah Kouleelawba. "He said it will be very dangerous," he inclined his head toward their leader, "and that only proves what I have always said about him: Spemica Lawba is a master of understatement."

"I do not expect or wish for you to join me in this undertaking," Spemica Lawba said. "Only keep watch out of sight and if something should happen to me, report to General Winchester with what we have learned."

Gituta's smile faded. "Do not mistake my joking for fear,

Spemica Lawba," he said. "The Otter does not admit to fear.
Besides . . . ," he glanced at Bright Horn, who nodded, and
Gituta's good humor returned, " . . . besides, everyone knows
you can't take care of yourself and need someone to watch over
you. We will come along."

Many of the Indians in the Tecumseh encampment were in
war paint and so the three painted themselves similarly, making
detection less likely. Hiding their horses in a ravine nearby, they
boldly strode into the camp and moved casually about, pausing
here and there to listen to conversations. So far as they could
determine, Tecumseh was not in the camp. All was going well
when suddenly a warrior who was squatting with others at one
of the fires followed his initial brief glance at them with a long
stare at Spemica Lawba.

He suddenly came to his feet pointing. "Spies!" he cried.
"These are spies! I know this one . . . he is —"

The words cut off as Spemica Lawba struck him full in the
face with his fist, not having realized until the man recognized
him that it was his uncle, Kumskaka. Staggering backward with
the blow, Kumskaka collided with another Indian just coming
to his feet and the two fell together.

"*Memequeluh!*" Spemica Lawba shouted — *Run!*

The three spies ran, heading toward the nearest copse of trees,
bowling over warriors who tried to bar their way and managing
to get a slight headstart before pursuit began in earnest. They
had entered the trees on the other side of the encampment from
where the horses had been hidden and now had to work their
way back to them. At one point he stopped his companions until
the pursuers were nearly upon them in the darkness and they
called out loudly in the Potawatomi dialect, "There they go! To
the north . . . the *north!* . . . Cut them off to the north!"

The pursuers sprinted away northward in the darkness and
the trio turned and ran south, circling the open encampment
and finally reaching the lower end of the ravine. Their horses
were nervous and whinnied loudly at their approach. They

quickly untied the animals and leaped on their backs. Already warriors were converging in their direction and a few shots were fired toward where the horses had been heard. They could hear the lead balls whistle past and clip twigs from the trees in their passage.

Leaning far forward, they urged the horses into a scrambling climb up the far side of the ravine and then they were galloping away, with the sounds of the pursuit quickly dwindling behind them. In a matter of four hours, they reached Fort Winchester, shouted the password when challenged, and were allowed to enter.

Within minutes they were at headquarters, reporting to General Winchester. They had hardly begun when a Kentucky officer, Major Samuel Price, entered and stood quietly near the door, listening as Johnny Logan gave a detailed accounting of what they had learned, concluding with their narrow escape from Tecumseh's encampment. As soon as the report was finished, General Winchester nodded approvingly.

"You're taking too many chances, Johnny. We don't want to lose you. You're too valu ——"

"Lies!" The single word from Major Price snapped like rifle shot in the room and they all stared at him. Spemica Lawba had never before met him and now his eyes narrowed dangerously, but Price went on. "General, that's a cock-and-bull story if I ever heard one. This Indian is making it all up. I believe he was in Tecumseh's camp, all right, no doubt about that. But I'll warrant he was there because he's one of Tecumseh's men. If he's a spy getting information for anyone, he's getting it for Tecumseh . . . *about us!*"

Spemica Lawba's hand had gone to the tomahawk in his belt, and had the accuser been another Indian, he would have killed him on the spot. Now he dropped his hand slowly away from the weapon, restraining himself only with extreme effort. His eyes had become dark ice and his words were brittle.

"Do not ever make such an accusation against me again, or I will kill you. Who are you to so accuse me?"

Price was unruffled, his tone of voice sneering. "I'm someone who won't be taken in by Indian tricks. I know precisely how treacherous you red niggers are! If I were the general, I'd order you taken out and hanged from the nearest —"

"Major!" Winchester had come to his feet, his eyes blazing. "Johnny Logan is one of our best spies. How *dare* you, sir, to come into this office and speak in such manner? Leave these quarters immediately and consider yourself under reprimand."

Major Price gave the commander a long insolent stare and opened the door. He paused and looked back. "General, he's the enemy, mark my words!" Then he was gone, the door closing loudly after him.

General Winchester, distressed, immediately apologized for his second's unwarranted attack, but Spemica Lawba was stung deeply. Never before in his career as a spy for the Americans had his fidelity been questioned. When the general was finished, the Shawnee drew himself up proudly and moved to the door.

"Ever since I was a boy," he said, "and adopted by General Benjamin Logan and given the name Johnny Logan by him, I have been faithful to the Americans. I made him this promise and I have never broken it, even though it meant separating from my family. I have been unjustly accused and so now I will prove my loyalty beyond any doubt . . . to you, to Major Price and to all other Americans. I will be back."

He had left then and immediately sought out his old friend William Oliver, who was at the fort. He told him what happened and then listened grimly as Oliver tried to argue him out of doing anything rash.

"Good Lord, Johnny," he said, "you don't have to prove a thing to Price. The man's a fool! He hates Indians — *all* Indians. He's blind with that hate. Forget Price. You're under no obligation to him."

Spemica Lawba shook his head. "My pride and my word are at stake. I'll start from here in the morning and either leave my bones bleaching in the woods or return with such trophies from the enemy that never again will any man accuse me of unfaithfulness."

He had planned to go alone, but Bright Horn and Otter would not hear of it. "It is our pride and honor, as well as yours, that are questioned," Otter said. "We will go."

"Yes," agreed Bright Horn. "You cannot deny us this."

So they left in the morning together, three days ago — November 22 — moving down the Maumee River, each with rifle, tomahawk and scalping knife. They traveled on foot, slowly, carefully. Despite this, about noon, while they had stopped to rest, they were surprised by a party of six mounted Potawatomies and a British officer. Spemica Lawba recognized the Indian in charge and the British officer. The latter was Matthew Elliott, British Indian agent and longtime friend of Simon Girty. The chief was none other than Winnemac.

Though covered by their guns, Spemica Lawba immediately came to his feet with a broad smile. He held out his hand and walked to them, shaking hands with both men he knew. "It's good to see you both again," he said in a very friendly manner. "I want you to meet my friends." He indicated his companions in turn, who also were standing now, taking their cue from Johnny and smiling. "This is Teopah Kouleelawba, who has been my friend since we were boys together. And this is Gituta, who has been my close friend for five summers."

"What are you doing here?" Elliott asked suspiciously, speaking fluently in the native tongue.

"These two and I," Johnny said lightly, "are tired of Americans. We have tried to live up to the Greenville Treaty and stay at peace with them, as our Chief Catahecassa remains, but we have come to believe they are dishonest and that they are, as Tecumseh has always warned, only interested in taking our lands. We have left them for good. Winnemac, you know that

Tecumseh is my uncle. Well, we are on our way now to throw ouselves behind Tecumseh and General Procter."

Winnemac grunted suspiciously and ordered the trio disarmed. He positioned men all around them and the whole group set out for the Rapids. Spemica Lawba took no offense at the treatment, but continued to chatter amiably with all of them as they walked. Gradually Winnemac relaxed and began to believe they were serious in their intentions to join Tecumseh. By the time the afternoon was half gone, he gave his warriors orders to restore their rifles.

The day was moving into dusk when they made camp on the bank of Turkeyfoot Creek, some twenty miles from Fort Winchester. Four of the Potawatomies ambled off in the nearby woods to search for some black haws before it became too dark and Spemica Lawba turned his head away from his captors and spoke in a whisper audible only to his two friends.

"This may be our only chance. Watch me. Shoot when I nod."

He stared up into a tree until, seeing this, Winnemac also looked up to discover what he was watching. Spemica Lawba nodded and instantly the three fired simultaneously. Winnemac and Matthew Elliott fell dead. The remaining warrior was knocked off his feet but only wounded. Even as he scrambled to get up, Spemica Lawba was reloading and as the warrior rushed him, shot him through the heart.

By this time shots were buzzing in at them from the four who had gone in search of black haws and had come running back at the sound of gunfire. Almost immediately one of their balls shattered Bright Horn's left shoulder, causing him to stagger and fall to one knee. The four Potawatomies had spread out and now had them in a crossfire, but Otter, his rifle reloaded, killed one, while Spemica Lawba scooped up the rifle of Matthew Elliott and killed another. Realizing that the odds had now shifted, the remaining two Potawatomies raced away, pausing in the gathering gloom long enough to reload and fire one more shot each toward the camp and then running again, this time without pause. They never even realized that one of these last two bullets had caught Spemica Lawba in the stomach, knocking him to a bent-over sitting position, his hands clasped about his middle.

Otter, unwounded, wasted no time. He helped Bright Horn up onto the back of Winnemac's horse, then gently lifted Spemica Lawba onto Elliott's. He was about to mount one of the remaining horses himself when Spemica Lawba called to him in a hoarse whisper.

"Gituta . . . *Gituta!* Their scalps . . . get them. It is . . . our proof."

Otter nodded and swiftly scalped the four dead men, stuffing the grisly trophies into a pouch on his waistband. Then he mounted and led them out. Moving along steadily, with both Bright Horn and Johnny Logan occasionally reeling and only barely keeping themselves from toppling, they reached Fort Winchester just after midnight.

Word quickly spread through the garrison that Johnny Logan's wound was very dangerous and might prove mortal. A pervading sadness filled the soldiers. Johnny Logan was well liked here and had long been a great favorite of theirs. The dislike most of them felt for General Winchester and the hatred for the newcomer, Major Price, intensified until it was a passion only thinly masked.

All through the next two days Spemica Lawba writhed in the extremes of his agony. He became delirious and comatose at intervals and not until only few minutes ago did his eyes open calmly and his gaze fall on his friend, William Oliver, seated beside the bed. Oliver's cheeks were wet and Spemica Lawba smiled slightly.

"Do not grieve, good friend," he whispered. "I am not sorry. I prize honor more than life. I die satisfied."

Oliver took his hand gently, holding it in both of his. The Shawnee closed his eyes but opened them again in a moment.

"My friend?"

"Yes, Johnny, I'm here. Right beside you."

"Go to Wapatomica. Tell Pskipacah Ouiskelotha that I . . . that I died as . . . a warrior. Tell . . . tell her that now I know that . . . Tecumseh . . ." He fell silent.

"What, Johnny. Tell her that Tecumseh what?"

"Tell her," his whisper had become croaky. "Tell . . . her that Tecumseh . . . was . . ." Again he stopped, eyes closed.

Oliver had long known of Johnny Logan's self-doubts and now he squeezed his Shawnee friend's hand hard without realizing it. "Johnny, what? Tell her that Tecumseh was what? Right? Wrong? Which?"

The eyes remained closed for a long while and breathing became raspy, but then the bloodless lips spread in a wide grin. Abruptly he laughed aloud, despite the pain it caused.

"What is it, Johnny?" Oliver asked softly.

Spemica Lawba opened his eyes again, rolling them toward his fellow scout. "I was . . . just remembering the unusual way Gituta . . . took the scalp . . . from Winnemac, while . . . while at the same time . . . looking . . . looking . . . looking in all directions." He laughed aloud again.

"How was he doing it, Johnny?"

There was no answer.

He was dead.

Spemica Lawba — also called Johnny Logan — was the only Indian in Ohio history to be buried with full military honors by officers and soldiers of the United States of America.